C0-ATJ-458

Christians for Biblical Equality
122 W Franklin Ave Ste 218
Minneapolis MN 55404-2451
Ph: 612-872-6898 Fax: 612-872-6891
Email: cbe@cbeinternational.org
Website: http://www.cbeinternational.org

sister stories

Daily Inspiration from the Lives of Ruth and Esther

WILLY NYWENING

CRC Publications
Grand Rapids, Michigan

Cover: © 1997 PhotoDisc, Inc.

© 1997 by CRC Publications, 2850 Kalamazoo Ave. SE, Grand Rapids, MI 49560. All rights reserved. With the exception of brief excerpts for review purposes, no part of this book may be reproduced in any manner whatsoever without written permission from the publisher. Printed in the United States of America on recycled paper. ✹ 1-800-333-8300 (US); 1-800-263-4252 (CAN)

Library of Congress Cataloging-in-Publication Data

Nywening, Willy, 1947-
    Sister stories: daily inspiration from the lives of
Ruth and Esther/Willy Nywening.
      p. cm.
    ISBN 1-56212-248-7
    1. Women—Prayer-books and devotions—English.
2. Devotional calendars. 3. Bible. O.T. Ruth—Devotional literature. 4. Bible. O.T. Esther Devotional
literature. I. Title.
BV4527.N88 1997
242'.5—dc21   96-18732
                                      CIP

10 9 8 7 6 5 4 3 2 1

With love for my daughters,

Elizabeth and Jennifer

contents

Preface 11

There Is a Time (Ruth 1:1-18)...........................12

Painful Anniversaries (Ruth 1:19-22)...................14

The Power of Love (Ruth 2:1-10).......................16

God's Wings (Ruth 2:11-16)..............................18

Daybreak (Ruth 2:19-23) 20

All the Colors of the Rainbow (Ruth 3:1-8) 22

Things Will Never Be the Same (Ruth 3:9-14)....24

Connections Beyond Cyberspace (Ruth 3:15-18)..............26

Putting Faith on the Line (Ruth 4:1-8) 28

Through a Child's Eyes (Ruth 4:9-12) 30

Better Than Seven Sons (Ruth 4:13-17)...............32

Our Mother's Voice (Ruth 4:13-22)....................34

Heads, Hair, and Sparrows (Esther 1:1-15) 36

A Fashion Statement (Esther 1:16-22) 38

Chosen (Esther 2:1-7)......................................40

Stay Away from the Water (Esther 2:8-11) 42

Wearing the Identity (Esther 2:10, 19-20)...........44

Beauty (Esther 2:12-18) 46

Have You Heard God Whisper? (Esther 2:19-23)..............48

Reflections in the Mirror (Esther 3:1-4) 50

Hearing the Bell (Esther 3:5-15).......................................52

The Right Place, the Right Time (Esther 4:1-14)...............54

Holding Hands (Esther 4:15-17) 56

Near to the Heart of God (Esther 4:15-16) 58

Dinner with the Lions (Esther 5:1-8) 60

Eating Pie (Esther 5:9-14) 62

No Coincidence (Esther 6:1-5) 64

Getting What We Deserve (Esther 6:6-14).........................66

Staying Warm (Esther 7) 68

Decisions and Socks (Esther 8:1-6) 70

MaryAnn and Her Cows (Esther 8:7-14) 72

Singing in the Streets (Esther 8:15-17) 74

Taking No Plunder (Esther 9:1-10)...................................76

Destroying a Tapeworm (Esther 9:11-17) 78

Peanut Butter Sandwiches (Esther 9:18-22) 80

Telling Our Stories (Esther 9:23-32).................................82

Happily Forever After (Esther 10) 84

preface

While the deeds and words, songs and prophecies of women are found in almost every part of the Bible, just two books are named after women and feature the stories of their lives. These are the books of Ruth and Esther.

Willy Nywening has taken these two Bible books and made them the basis for a number of meditations that bring the past into the present and relate the stories of these ancient sisters to the life issues facing women today. Ruth's steadfast devotion to her mother-in-law and her mother-in-law's God led her through poverty into a new life of prosperity and peace; she becomes a model of how love and trust should permeate our family living. Esther's faith and courage in facing possible death for the sake of her threatened people brought new life and hope to them all; her example should encourage us to make the right choices and decisions about the course of our own lives.

It is our prayer that these Sister Stories may inspire you also to walk faithfully with your God.

Harvey A. Smit
Editor in chief
Education, Worship, & Evangelism Department

there is a time

READ RUTH 1:1-18 & ECCLESIASTES 3:1-8.

It's hard to remember how happy I was back in the beginning, back in those days when Mahlon and I were first married. My friends all thought I was crazy. "You don't want to marry that foreigner," they told me. " He's not of our race. He comes from a different culture. He doesn't think the way we do." I knew they were right. Marriage is tough enough without overcoming some of the problems Mahlon and I would face. But I knew there was something special about him and his family. And I wanted to be one of them—no matter what my friends and family said.

Mahlon and I were happy during our years together—in spite of what my friends predicted. His brother, Killion, had married a Moabite too, a friend of mine named Orpah. So I wasn't the only Moabite in the family. The four of us had a lot of fun together, and I think we brought happiness to Naomi, my mother-in-law, too. She had some sad times, some down times, remembering Elimilech her husband, who had died shortly after they arrived in Moab. But her sons could still make her eyes crinkle with joy.

That joy vanished altogether when Mahlon and Killion died. At first I was so overwhelmed by my own grief that I didn't even see Naomi's. I cried for days, unable to eat or sleep. But as I gradually worked through my grief, I began to notice that Naomi wasn't herself. The triple loss of her husband and two sons seemed to be more than she could bear.

Then came the day of her big decision. Orpah and I had just come from the market when we saw her standing by the door. "I have something to tell you," she said. "I've decided to go home, back to the land of my God and my people. I love you both, but it's time that I move on. Soon you will find new husbands who will make you happy again."

Orpah caught my eye, and I knew she was thinking the same thing I was thinking: Naomi could never make this long journey on her own. If she was determined to go back to Judah, we would have to go with her.

At first Naomi protested. But gradually she weakened. What Orpah and I said made sense, and she knew it. We were young and strong.

She was frail from grief and age. The trip would be much easier if we went together.

The trip wasn't a pleasant one. We had a lot to carry, it was hot, and Naomi's spirits were still very low. Often we walked side by side, quietly, each deep in our own thoughts.

One day we stopped by an oasis, and I saw a look of determination put steel back into Naomi's eyes. "Come and sit," she said to me and Orpah. "I have something to tell you." We found a spot under a tall tree and sat together in the sand. "I have thought long and hard," Naomi began, "and I really think it's best if you two go back to your own homes." She frowned as she told us the things she had been worrying about—that if we went on with her our chance of remarrying was very slim. "There's no love lost between your race and mine," she reminded us. "If you come home with me, you're going to face prejudice and discrimination every day of your lives. People will despise you, look down on you. They may not let you worship with us or attend our celebrations. I'm afraid you'll never be happy."

The three of us hugged each other and cried together. Then Orpah shook her head yes. "I think you're right, Naomi. I think I should return to Moab," she said. "We're close enough to Judah now. You can travel the rest of the way alone."

But not me. My heart broke at the thought of leaving this woman I loved, this woman I had learned to call mother. There was something special about her and her God—something important and wonderful that I knew I wanted for myself. "I'll go wherever you go, Naomi," I said. "Your people will be my people. Your God will be my God. . . ."

That was a long time ago now. I'm a grandmother many times over, and I have more time to think than I used to. I know now how important that decision I made that day was. I had to make a tough choice, and somehow God led me to make the right one. And then God blessed me—in amazing ways!

It's such a great story that I have told it again and again. "Next time you move into a time of decision," I say to the people I know, "trust God! God will bless you in wonderful, unimaginable ways."

What a great God we have!

PRAYER

Jesus, thank you for the story of Ruth. Thank you for her courage. Help me to learn from her example. Teach me to make good choices for you. I thank you that you are in control of my life. Amen.

FOLLOW-UP

Read and enjoy the entire story of Ruth.

painful anniversaries

READ RUTH 1:19-22 & PSALM 103.

As the "branding iron" of humiliation sizzled and left its mark, the silence in the church was disturbed only by the soft muffled crying of a mother. Two of my friends were standing at the front of the church confessing their sin. They "had to get married." They were teenagers, children themselves, thrust into marriage because they were pregnant. It was considered the right thing to do under the circumstances. It would make the baby legitimate. It would awkwardly camouflage the shame.

As young people learning the facts of life, we had calculated the months from the date of our parents' anniversaries to the birth of their first child. For some it had been a shocking and humiliating revelation. We found it difficult to accept that any of our births had been an accident. We vowed it would never happen to any of us. When it did, it was beyond our comprehension. It was a knife that cut through our innocence, our self-esteem, and our friendships.

You could literally hear a pin drop as the minister solemnly asked the young couple if they were sorry for their sin. We had discussed this question in our innermost circles. We knew

they had to be repentant. Unfortunately, we believed their remorse was more for getting caught than for the actual deed. Even now, thirty years later, as I recall that scene, I can hear and feel the pain and humiliation that that congregation and its leaders inflicted. The joy and gift of this couple's child would be tainted by the humiliation and guilt that they felt. Anniversaries would be painful and carefully camouflaged.

The fear that those confessions instilled in the teens who watched was beyond description. It was without a doubt the thing we least wanted to happen to us. Yes, we knew and believed what the Bible said, but the reality was that the best reason for avoiding premarital sex was the sure and certain knowledge that we would stand at the front of the church to be married and marked forever with the label, "But they had to get married, you know." Humiliation, guilt, and fear of rejection hung over the heads of those who had knowingly broken the seventh commandment. We had learned well to be ashamed of our sins, but we had not been taught that God's forgiveness and acceptance will heal the wounds and allow us to move on.

Thankfully, we no longer subject our youth to this horrendous discipline. But unfortunately many other violations of God's law still stigmatize people. Addiction, divorce, abortion, and venereal diseases are transgressions that have degraded many. Today, these sins can still shame us; however, AIDS seems to be the most feared "branding iron" of the nineties.

In Ruth's world there were many things to fear too—especially for women. One of the branding irons of that culture was the title "childless widow"—a fate dreaded above all others. A childless widow had no status, no land, and worst of all, no one to carry on the family name. The doctor might as well have told her she had AIDS.

It was this hopeless situation that Naomi faced. Her husband and sons were dead, and she was too old to have more children. She came back to Judah an empty, bitter, broken woman who would have to depend on the kindness of others to live out her life. She believed and accepted that God had punished and cursed her. In her emptiness she could not celebrate any of the anniversaries of her life.

Was Naomi right? Was she being punished for fleeing to Moab with her husband and sons instead of staying in Judah and trusting God? Is the pain and loneliness and grief we experience in our lives God's way of punishing us, of saying "I told you so"? Is it God's way of disciplining wayward children?

In Psalm 103 we see that, like the mother who cried during the confession of my friends, God feels our pain and weeps with us. God finds no pleasure in our grief and pain, our mistakes and our suffering. So God told Naomi, "Your actions have consequences that you must own. But because you love me, I will turn those tragedies into blessings. I will make you whole, and I will fill your life."

God gives us the same assurance. Whatever shame or pain we carry with us, God tells us to let it go, to leave it behind.

And then God fills our lives with celebrations of grace.

PRAYER

Thank you for your perfect love for me. God, you know there are times when guilt and fear rule my life. Help me to accept your forgiveness. Help me to forgive myself. Teach me to love you and to live by your law. Amen.

FOLLOW-UP

Think of a favorite song of praise that expresses your love for God. Lift your heart, your head, and your hands and sing it.

the power of love

READ RUTH 2:1-10 & 1 CORINTHIANS 13.

The old man bravely struggled to hold back his tears. The kind, selfless words of his grandson had overwhelmed him.

Others could have told him that he shouldn't have been surprised. The boy had grown up with an excellent example of selfless giving—the old man himself. It was Opa [Grandpa] who had patiently baited his fishhook again and again. Opa who had always had time to read to him and walk and talk with him and fix his flat tires. Opa who had slept on the ground in a tent, at the age of seventy-eight, because he knew how much the boy and his brother wanted to camp with him once more.

And now, Opa had been told that his kidneys had failed. He would have to spend the rest of his life dependent on a kidney dialysis machine to clean his blood and to stay alive. The boy listened intently as the details were explained. The realization that life would be so much different now for this strong, seemingly ageless man began to dawn on the boy.

"Why can't you get a transplant, Opa?" the boy asked.

"When you're eighty, you're too old for a kidney transplant. Besides, there are too many young people who need kidneys," replied Opa gently.

The fourteen-year-old wrapped his long, lanky arms around his beloved Opa, surrounding him with himself and said, "Then I'll give you one of my kidneys, Opa. I don't need them both."

The man's love and kindness had come full circle. All his defenses were swept away, and he wept shamelessly.

Ruth's love surrounded Naomi in the same way. She had refused to leave her mother-in-law when she wanted to come home. She had half carried Naomi back to her beloved Bethlehem. And now she would do whatever was necessary to take care of Naomi and keep her safe. The women were poor and destitute. Their prospects were not good. There were few honorable options for surviving.

There was, however, a Jewish law that provided a type of food bank that could help them stay alive. During the harvest time, the poor, the alien, the widow, and the fatherless were allowed to pick up or glean the grain that was dropped or left on the fields after the workers were finished harvesting the crop. This was a reputable way for the destitute to feed themselves. When Ruth became aware of this law, she asked Naomi for permission to go and glean.

Ruth probably also knew that not all landowners respected this law of Moses. And she may have heard that sometimes, even if the landowners allowed gleaners to be in the fields, their workers resented people getting things for nothing. They often would be less than kind or understanding to a gleaner—especially a foreign, pretty, single woman. So there was a distinct possibility that she would be harassed or taken advantage of. Yet, without hesitation Ruth set out to find a field in which to glean, "behind anyone in whose eyes I find favor."

Just when it looks as if things couldn't get much worse for Naomi and Ruth, Ruth found herself in the field of Boaz, a relative of Naomi's, a well-to-do landowner. As she worked, he approached her. Fear of what he might say or do must have gripped her, but she respectfully requested permission to glean in his field. Much to her surprise, he welcomed her and ensured her comfort and safety by allowing her to drink the water of his own servant girls and by making sure that none of his workers harmed her in any way.

Like Opa, Ruth was overwhelmed by the kindness shown to her. But she shouldn't have been surprised. Her actions had exemplified how the law should be kept. The love she had freely given to Naomi was now returned by Boaz.

Yes, they'll know we are Christians by our love.

PRAYER

Thank you, Jesus, for loving me. Thank you for the people in my life who love and care for me. Make me strong and courageous in my caring for others. Help me to be an instrument of your love.

FOLLOW-UP

Spend an hour visiting a shut-in. Bring flowers or a small gift. Expect no recognition or thanks.

God's wings

READ RUTH 2:11-16 & PSALM 4.

Dear Orpah,

The strangest and yet the most wonderful things have happened since you left us.

It was really difficult at first. The closer we got to Bethlehem, the more depressed Naomi seemed. She kept saying, "God is punishing me. I should have known better." I didn't know how to comfort her. It was so hard to understand what was so wonderful about a God who would let your husband and your sons die and leave you all alone. One day I asked her about it. All she said was, "God works in strange ways. He will take care of us."

When we got to Bethlehem, things got worse. Her old friends were happy to see her, but they had that "I told you so" look in their eyes. They were polite in front of Naomi, but I heard some of them whispering about me. I knew that fitting in wouldn't be easy, but I wasn't prepared for the treatment I got—even though Naomi had warned me it might happen. Nobody talked to me. They acted like I didn't even exist. You can't imagine how lonely I felt.

I have to admit that I'm learning more and more about how much the Jews hate the Moabites. For a while there, I cried myself to sleep every night. I kept trying to remember what Naomi had said about her God working in strange ways, but the snubs and sneers hurt just the same.

Sometimes as I lay awake, I talked to Naomi's God. Naomi told me that's what God expects people to do. She said it would help me. At first I really didn't know what to say in my prayers. So I decided I might as well be honest. I told God everything. I even talked about how angry I was that God had let all these terrible things happen to Naomi and me. I don't know why or how, but I always feel better after talking to this God. It's so much different than talking to the gods back home.

I didn't tell Naomi how awful I was feeling during those weeks and months. She was so hungry and tired all the time that I couldn't see adding to her burdens. Instead I tried to get my mind off our troubles by thinking of ways that we could get some money. Remember when Naomi first talked about going home? She told us that her God was providing food for his people. Well, that's not as simple as it sounded. We quickly found out that it costs *money* to buy food, and we didn't have any.

At first I thought we'd starve to death, but then I learned about an interesting Jewish law that allows the poor to glean in the fields. I thought that might be a solution to our food problem. But when I mentioned it to some of Naomi's friends, they got this strange look in their eyes. No one would explain. They just said, "Be careful!"

I went to one of the fields closest to where we are living. As I started walking behind the workers, picking up little bits of grain, I saw a well-dressed, obviously important, man walking in the field. I noticed how friendly he was to all the workers. Even so, I was scared that he wouldn't be happy to see a foreign woman gleaning in his field. But, Orpah, the most wonderful thing happened! He welcomed me. Can you believe it?

I was so shocked that I said the first thing that came to my mind: I asked him why he would be so nice to a Moabite. You'll never believe what he said. He told me he had heard about Naomi and me. And he said the strangest thing. He called on his God to reward me. The God under whose wings I have taken refuge. I didn't understand this at all. But, all of a sudden I *did* feel safe and protected—both by God and by this man.

I told the man how much his words meant to me. Then, believe it or not, he invited me to join his servants for lunch. I haven't eaten so much in weeks! I even had enough food so I could take some home for Naomi.

When I went back to the fields to glean in the afternoon, I was sure that people were looking at me differently. One of the other girls was actually friendly. Not only that, but there seemed to be a lot more wheat left on the fields. I wonder if the workers were leaving more on purpose?

There are so many things I don't understand about these people and this God. If everything Naomi has told me is true, then this man, Boaz, must have some special connection to the God of the Jews. He is so different from most of the others. . . .

Can it be that *he* is the wings of God?

Love,

Ruth

PRAYER

Lord, thank you for your wings that cover me. Thank you for the people that show me your love. Thank you for people that I am safe with. Help me to learn how to be your wings. Amen.

FOLLOW-UP

Write a note to someone who has been God's wings in your life. Tell the person how he or she has helped you to know God. Thank the person for the refuge he or she provides in your life.

daybreak

READ RUTH 2:19-23 & HEBREWS 6:13-20.

"You don't know what it means to be hungry."

Whenever there were complaints in our family about being hungry, these words were sure to admonish us. The occupation of The Netherlands and the deprivation it caused haunted my parents. They had witnessed the desperation of those who could not find food to keep their children alive. They had watched and endured as the hunger demon stripped the flesh and eventually life from loved ones who were too weak to endure. Together with so many others, they had battled with the monster as it tried to rob them of their dignity and purpose.

We had heard the stories. The tales of how tulip bulbs were dug up, dried, and ground up for flour. As children, we thought that the accounts of how cats and dogs were eaten as a last resort were preposterous. In a home where there was always food, it was impossible for us to imagine the despair that hunger brought during those horrendous times. It was inconceivable to me that things could be that desperate.

When I heard those stories, I sometimes wondered how the country was able to survive. Why didn't they give up when they were being choked into submission? Why did they keep resisting the onslaught of the enemy? My mother provided the answer. She explained that the war was like the night. It was dark and sometimes very frightening, but it had to end because God had promised that the day would follow the night. The belief that the Allies would come was like the conviction that the morning follows the night. My mother explained that without the hope that freedom would dawn again, many people would have found life not worth living. It would be like going to bed and not believing that there would be a next day. Although I didn't really understand the analogy, it made sense to me. I knew that hope had empowered the human spirit.

World War II ended fifty years ago. But many forms of suffering and evil continue to darken our world. Globally, there is sickness, disaster, and war. Like the war I was told about, these catastrophes can seem far removed from my everyday life. But sometimes the horrors are much more subtle and closer to home. Despair can come in packages of many sizes and shapes. It can be wrapped neatly in rejection, control, abuse, and injustice. It can be discreetly camouflaged in supposedly safe places and seemingly loving relationships. It can blanket me and leave me isolated, cold, and alone. Then desperation becomes the enemy that I must battle.

When hopelessness wraps itself around us, we may react with the same despair that Naomi did when she lost her family. To her this curse was like a demon that had consumed her life and left a dark, empty hole. She was just going through the motions, wallowing in the darkness, in the quicksand of the night. When we are without the hope, the belief, that life can be reclaimed, many afflictions can ravage us too. They can chew us up, spit us out, and leave us for dead. Then hope must be the lifeline that keeps us from drowning.

Until she heard of Boaz, Naomi had been devoured by her feelings. They had consumed her life and left it empty. When she dared to believe there might be a kinsman-redeemer, someone capable of rescuing her from drowning in the muck, she was able to begin the journey to solid ground. She could see a glimmer of the dawn on the horizon. As she began to hope and believe her night would end, a new day could start to break.

When things were at their worst, Naomi reached out and claimed the promise. You and I can do the same.

"We have this hope as an anchor for the soul, firm and secure. It enters the inner sanctuary behind the curtain, where Jesus, who went before us, has entered on our behalf" (Hebrews 6: 19-20).

PRAYER

Thank you that your light makes my nights turn into day. Teach me to hope in you and reach out to you. Make me humble enough to reach out for help when I need it. Where there's despair in life, empower me to bring your hope. Where there is darkness, teach me to bring your light. Amen.

FOLLOW-UP

Identify a situation that feels hopeless in your life. Pray for help to confront it. Identify and reach out to someone who is empowered to be a "kinsman-redeemer" for you. Deal with the despair.

all the colors of the rainbow

Faith is all the colors of the rainbow,
the arc that covers and connects the jagged
corners of my life—
　　red for His blood, the starting point,
　　orange for courage and daring,
　　yellow for renewal and hope,
　　green for the new beginnings of growth,
　　blue for the cold of hurts,
　　purple for the promise of greatness.
Faith is wearing,
　　being the colors as they drape my life.
Faith is knowing all things are possible
　　as I embrace and color myself complete
　　in Him.

A rainbow is simply sunlight, broken up into different colors as it hits the surface of a drop of water. The curved inner surface of the drop acts like a mirror that reflects the colors to our eyes.

I'm glad that I don't need to know the scientific explanation to appreciate the magnificent beauty of a rainbow. It brilliantly paints hope across the sky after a storm has unleashed its fury on us. It radiates with the promise of God's faithfulness to his people—a promise that isn't diminished in any way because my precise knowledge and understanding of this natural phenomena is limited.

And so it is with faith. I may not understand it completely or be able to explain it exactly to know that it is real. But I can experience it, hold on to it, and let its colors permeate my life.

Stones can be like a rainbow. They hold a promise. By themselves they are quite dead and often useless. But if I pick them up and strike them together, they will release a spark that can set the world on fire. However, this mystery will only take place if I believe that it is possible and act on my conviction. Then, all the colors of the rainbow will break out of the hopelessness of a stagnant stone and light up my being.

Once Naomi's faith and hope is rekindled by the spark of Boaz's kindness, she picks up the flints and moves to light the fire. Now that she believes a new beginning is possible, she takes action. There can be a name, a future for Ruth if she boldly claims the promise given in the law of Moses. Naomi knows what Ruth must do. She must wash and perfume herself and put on her best dress. Then she must go and lay at the feet of Boaz as he protects his grain on the threshing floor. What Ruth is really instructed to do is to petition Boaz to act on his obligation as a relative. In other words, Ruth must propose marriage to Boaz. Although this seems like quite a daring thing to ask Ruth to do, Naomi is simply picking up the fire stones and striking them. She knows and believes that if something is to happen, she must act. Wrapped in the colors of the rainbow, she lights the fire.

Boldly wearing her own colors of faith, Ruth does exactly what Naomi says to do. She doesn't question Naomi, or ask for reasons, or protest that such behavior might be dangerous or improper. She goes to the threshing floor (a place women are seldom seen), and she hides.

She watches Boaz having a good time. When she sees that he has finished eating and drinking and has made himself comfortable at the far end of the grain floor, she quietly slips in, uncovers his feet, and lays down.

What a wonderful exhibition of complete and total trust!

A uniquely beautiful, simple portrait of faith is painted for us in this story of Ruth and Naomi. Two seemingly simple women, the lowest of the low in their society, teach us what faith is. In Hebrews 11, we read of many others who modeled and acted on their faith. They trusted that the impossible or improbable would happen. And it did.

Faith is all the colors of the rainbow.

PRAYER

Thank you, Jesus, for rainbows. Thank you for your promise of faith, hope, and love. Teach me to trust you completely. Teach me to hold your hand and then to walk on water. Forgive me when I forget that anything is possible with you. Amen.

FOLLOW-UP

As an act of faith, plant some flower seeds. Believe and know that they will grow. As they grow, be encouraged to act on your faith in simple, meaningful ways.

things will never be the same

READ RUTH 3:9-14 & ACTS 4:32-36

Picture a huge pair of scissors. Watch as they easily snip through your job, your pension, your health care, your vacation, and just about anything else that costs money. . . .

We call it downsizing. All over the world governments and businesses are picking up their slicing instrument and brutally attacking the cost of operating. Across North America one company after another announces layoffs and closings. Some governments are going so far as suggesting they may have to declare bankruptcy.

The arms and hands of social programs are often among the first to be amputated from the priority list. As government assistance dwindles, pleas go out across the media for us to be more generous in our giving to local food banks and publicly-funded charities. Foundations hire fund-raisers who conduct telephone surveys and appeal to the public to be more benevolent towards those who are less fortunate. We hear horror stories of the elderly who are slowly starving because their pensions are too small to provide for their needs. We walk through our city streets and encounter beggars on every corner, beseeching us with, "Can you spare some change?" And sometimes we self-righteously shake our heads and wonder where we are headed. We ask, "What's the world coming to, and where will it all end?"

Everyone has a reason and a solution for our current state of affairs. Some blame the rich for being greedy. "Why don't they pay more taxes?" Some blame the poor for being lazy. "Why don't they get a job?" Some blame politicians for overspending. "Didn't they think about what would happen in the long run?" Some blame the moral decline in our society. "When we were young, we wouldn't have thought of doing such things." Some blame feminists for destroying the fabric of the family. "All mothers should stay home and look after their families." And the finger-pointing could go on and on and on.

It's easy to join the chorus of complainers. But one day the scissors may cut into our lives. And suddenly it will become really important for someone to bandage the hurt, someone to answer the questions. . . .

And still the scissors keep cutting. Despite the outbursts and the finger-pointing, it seems that the turmoil in our world, in our communities, continues to get worse.

For Ruth and Naomi the social order of the day did not provide assistance of any kind. The law of Moses offered the only safety net for the disenfranchised. And like our social programs today, it faced cuts and had many holes to fall through. It was also flawed by people and governments who had overextended themselves. These people had been at war, they had been struggling with their religious-belief system, with their priorities, with who they were as a people of God. They had their own kind of downsizing. The *NIV Study Bible* states that the book of Ruth was set in the time of the Judges. This was "a period of religious and moral degeneracy, national disunity, and general foreign oppression." Sound familiar?

And in the midst of all that chaos, one person says to an abandoned family, "I will do it." He will do it because he sees it as his obligation as a relative. He will do it because it is his duty. He will do it willingly, without complaining that the other, closer relative should do it. He will do it selflessly. That profound act of kindness changes the course of his nation. It changes history for you and for me. Boaz commits to fulfilling his responsibility. He does it because it is right and honorable. He does it because it is the response God would have him make.

As the shears continue to make incisions in our society, you and I must also find a way to say, "I will do it." Things will never be the same again.

PRAYER

Jesus, thank you for the society I live in. Thank you for freedom and for help when times are bad. Teach me what my responsibility is. Show me how I can make a difference. Help me, encourage me to make it. Amen.

FOLLOW-UP

Identify a single parent who could use your help. Make a list of simple things you could do for the person (example: babysitting for an hour or two a week). Commit to helping the person in small, meaningful ways. (If you are a single parent, choose someone with less time and fewer resources than you have.)

connections beyond cyberspace

READ RUTH 3:15-18 & JOHN 19:25-27.

Would you like to meet me in cyberspace?

Today millions of people are getting together through the telephone connections of their computer modems that in effect allow computers to talk to each other on conventional telephone lines. Electronic mail, or E-mail, is the postal system of the nineties. Computer users with a basic Internet connection and a personal E-mail address can connect instantly with anyone, anywhere in the world. With a click on a mouse, letters can be transmitted thousands of miles into the mailboxes of family, friends, and even strangers.

Through the Internet, I communicate daily with my daughters who are far away at school. It is comforting and reassuring for me to be able to talk to them, to chat about the everyday things that are happening in their lives and mine.

What a small world we live in! Not only can we talk to any part of the world at any time, but we can also see history developing around the world through television satellites that bring the events right into our living rooms.

Through the media of the Internet, television, and telephone we are able to form connections to people around the world. This amazing technology of the twentieth century has enabled a completely new definition of community to emerge. We can know what is happening far away, and we are able to take part almost instantly in the celebrations, joys, and sorrows of those we care about. Our homes have become places in which we are able to connect with our immediate family and friends, as well as with many others around the world.

Although they would not be able to fathom the technology, Naomi and Ruth certainly knew about being connected. Their extended family was the entire nation of Israel. They were bound together by common beliefs and the parentage of Abraham—bonds every bit as strong and immediate as the invisible links of the Internet. Naomi knew that she was part of a distinct, chosen nation that was held together by a covenant, a promise that tied them firmly to God. She took hold of those cords and tied herself and Ruth firmly to the family and to the God in whom they were anchored.

The incredible technology of today enables me to be linked to my family and friends in strange and wonderful ways. In some ways it has made my world much smaller. Because the Internet is so vast, it also reminds me of the safety and security of small places. In my home I can be myself. I can kick off my shoes, put on my jeans, take off my makeup, and put my feet on the table. Home is the place where someone will ask me how my day was or how I'm feeling. It's the place where I am loved, valued, and given a hug when I need it.

Most of us do not choose our immediate family. Ruth did. She made a conscience decision to be part of Naomi's family. Their world was very small, and their immediate family was only a group of two, but they nurtured and cared for each other. When Ruth came back from the threshing floor, she must have been bursting with excitement. I'm sure she couldn't wait to tell Naomi about how scared she was when she was proposing to Boaz and how wonderful she felt when he reacted honorably.

Families and communities are an important part of our everyday lives. We need people to interact with, people who will listen to our fears and our triumphs. We need to have people who will be there for us, who won't let us down. Sometimes we can find the fulfillment of those needs in our traditional families. But for many different reasons, traditional families break down. Then, like Ruth and Naomi, we need to find extended, diverse families where we can cultivate relationships that support and sustain us.

You and I may never talk to each other on the Internet. But our belief in a risen Lord ties us together in a much stronger and more incredible way. We will certainly meet beyond cyberspace in a heavenly place.

PRAYER

Thank you, Father, for the incredible technology of today. Thank you for the many people who make up your family. Help me to feel connected to others who love and serve you. Help me to be a supportive part of the communities you give me. Amen.

FOLLOW-UP

Send a letter to a missionary. Connect with the person in a real and meaningful way. Tell the person that you will pray for her/him as part of your Christian community.

putting faith on the line

READ RUTH 4:1-8 & ROMANS 5:1-5.

Kathy's heart began to pound loudly as she felt the moisture dripping on her thigh. She was eleven weeks pregnant, and she knew instinctively what the fluid meant: the life of her unborn child was in danger. She rushed to the hospital where the doctor confirmed her fears. The placenta of the baby was covering the mouth of the uterus, causing critical hemorrhaging. The good news was that the baby's heart was still beating. The bad news was that a miscarriage seemed likely.

The doctor tried his best to be optimistic. It *might* be possible to save the baby, he said, but complete bed rest would be imperative. Kathy would need to remain in the hospital until the bleeding stopped and then rest at home. Kathy rebelled at the idea of being separated from the two young daughters (ages two years and eight months old) who needed her at home. But she agreed to give the doctor's "prescription" a try.

Several weeks passed. The bleeding continued. The specialists confirmed that although the baby was still alive, there was a great risk to the child and to Kathy. The placenta could suddenly break away from the uterus wall. The woman could quickly bleed to death. They recommended an abortion to terminate the pregnancy. They reasoned that Kathy had two other small children who needed her. And she could have other children if she chose. There was absolutely no need to risk her life.

Tears streamed down Kathy's face as she listened to the doctor tell her that she ought to move on with her life. She had listened to the heartbeat of the child daily. In spite of her impatience with laying in bed and being separated from her other children, Kathy believed that her unborn child deserved a chance to live.

"I can't do it," she told the doctor. "I'm going to have this baby." With the support of her husband and her family doctor, Kathy chose to put the life of her unborn child and her own life in God's hands. She chose to ignore the specialists who told her she was taking a selfish, foolish, unnecessary risk.

The specialists or elders of Boaz's town probably thought the same thing when Boaz said he was going to marry Ruth. After Ruth proposed to Boaz, he went to the town gate, the business office of the day, and asked

Naomi's closest relative if he wished to redeem Elimelech's land according to the Hebrew law. The death of Elimilech and his sons provided an unusual opportunity for the kinsman to acquire more land. If Naomi had no other heirs, the land could be assumed by the kinsman's own sons. Any everyone knew Naomi was too old to have more children.

But then Boaz reminded the kinsman of the second requirement of the law. The kinsman must also marry Naomi's daughter-in-law, the Moabitess Ruth. According to the law, this would mean the first son born to the kinsman and Ruth would actually be the son of Mahlon. This provision protected a family name that would otherwise die out. It also meant that if there was only one son, he would inherit all of his father's property. In other words, the relative could end up being in the same situation that Naomi was in. By marrying Ruth, he could be jeopardizing his own family name. So from the human perspective, claiming the land and marrying Ruth was an unwise gamble. It just wasn't worth the risk.

The kinsman said to Boaz, "Buy the land yourself if you want to chance it; I can't do it."

Like the kinsman, Boaz knew that buying the land and marrying Ruth would be a costly and foolhardy venture, especially since she wasn't even a Jew. But Boaz saw things that the kinsman missed. He recognized Ruth's faith and commitment, and he called on God to bless her for her devotion and kindness. Perhaps that is one reason he was not afraid to put his name on the line, to risk everything and take her for his wife. How wonderful that God blessed them both for trusting him!

Kathy was blessed too. She gave birth to a normal, healthy, baby boy. He is now a strong young man. Yet every night when he is sleeping she still tiptoes into his room, kisses him gently, and thanks God for the miracle of his birth.

PRAYER

Dear Jesus, help me to turn my problems over to you and to have faith in your will for my life. Give me strength to face difficulties. Help me to remember that there are no accidents or mistakes in your perfect will. Amen.

FOLLOW-UP

Think of an area in your life about which you are doubtful or uncertain. Write a letter to God asking for help. Trust that God will answer it in his perfect plan.

through a child's eyes

READ RUTH 4:9-12 & MARK 5:24-34.

A riddle for you to solve:

What has all the magnificent colors of the
*   rainbow,*
appears and disappears almost mysteriously,
is always shaped the same
yet each time is a different surprise,
is as light as air and as delicate as a crystal
*   figurine,*
yet is wonderfully strong, full and complete,
is so exquisitely beautiful and delicate, adults
*   marvel at it,*
yet is so simple a child can create it?

The enjoyment that young children receive from the simplest pleasures amazes me. When they are young, they seldom ask for elaborate explanations. They sit and repeat the same uncomplicated task over and over. It can be putting together a puzzle, making a structure with blocks, or blowing bubbles. Yes, that's one of the answers to the riddle.

Have you ever watched as children blow bubbles? They sit patiently, intently exhaling to produce little circles of perfection. They marvel at the shades of transparent colors and watch intently as they float into the air. Often, there is a real sense of awe, followed by utterances of delight as each delicate sphere drifts into the atmosphere and disappears. Children may also enjoy bursting bubbles. There is something wonderful and innocent about this entire activity. The reward for blowing bubbles is the pure, simple pleasure it creates.

In the same uncomplicated way children see such simple pleasures, we can sometimes see miracles. Miracles are marvelous, surprising events created by God. Think about Ruth's marriage to Mahlon, Ruth's refusal to leave Naomi, the marriage of Ruth and Boaz, and the birth of their son. These happenings were all most unlikely. There were not just chance occurrences of fate. They were miracles. Gifts bestowed by a loving, gracious, forgiving God. Ruth didn't know the fancy words that the priests prayed. Her conviction was simple and uncomplicated. Her trust was like that of an unpretentious child who innocently creates exquisite bubbles.

The elders of Bethlehem recognized what a special event the union of Ruth and Boaz was. They blessed Ruth and Boaz by calling on God to make them famous. They asked that God would make Ruth like Rachel and Leah, the wives of Jacob who were the mothers of all the tribes of Israel. They also wished her standing in Ephrathah and fame in Bethlehem like that of Tamar and her husband, Perez, who had helped to make Judah the most important tribe in Israel.

The blessings offered to Ruth and Boaz came to partial fulfillment in the birth of their great-grandson, David, who became king of the Hebrew nation. They came to complete realization and fulfillment in the birth of Jesus Christ. The gift of that miracle in Bethlehem so many years later makes it possible for us to share in the same blessing.

In a pressing crowd, an outcast, a desperate woman much like Ruth, seeks out the Lord. She is sick, frightened, and desperate, but she is sure of what she wants and how she will get it. The woman reaches out to touch Jesus' coat, and a miracle happens. The woman's faith is simple, yet strong, full, and complete. It is enough for the Master to acknowledge and affirm it. It is enough for her to be healed and given the gift of peace.

Bubbles take a childlike expectation to be created, seen, and appreciated. Miracles are like that too. With childlike faith, our eyes will see them.

PRAYER

Thank you, Jesus, for the examples of faith in your book, the Bible. I ask you for that same simple faith. Help me to believe that miracles are possible. Open my eyes so that I will see them. Amen.

FOLLOW-UP

Enjoy blowing some bubbles. Do it with a child or by yourself. As you watch the bubbles, pray that God will give you the childlike faith needed to see the miracles around you. Give thanks for the miracles that God has already provided in your life.

better than seven sons

READ RUTH 4:13-17 & P.SALM 40.

Dear Obed,
Today I feel like a pitcher that is full and overflowing with cool, refreshing water. It is a beautiful, sunny, warm day—the day you were circumcised. Now you belong to God. As I held you in my arms and rocked you to sleep this afternoon, I wanted to tell you so many things. I am an old woman, and by the time you are able to understand the wonder of your birth, I believe I may be with the Lord. So I will write you a letter.

First, let me tell you about Mahlon, your mother's first husband, and Elimilech, my husband. It's important that you know about them, because you bear their name and will one day inherit their land.

Things were not always as good as they are now in Israel. Several years before you were born, times were very difficult. So Elimilech and I decided to move to the land of Moab, where the future appeared to be brighter. My husband and I packed up our things and went looking for a better future for our two sons, Mahlon and Killion. At first, all went well. Mahlon married your mother, Ruth, and

Killion married another young woman, Orpah. We were very happy and content. I hoped that there would soon be grandchildren for me to look after.

Then, catastrophe struck. Within a very short time my husband and my two sons died. I felt that my life had been taken and poured out onto the ground. I was left completely empty. And I came to the conclusion that God was punishing me. I must admit to you that I turned into a bitter, angry woman.

In my anger and grief I decided that I needed to come home and die in my own country. Your mother and Orpah insisted on coming with me—even though I didn't think it was a good idea. When we were getting close to Israel, Orpah returned to Moab, but your mother absolutely refused to leave me. So we traveled to Bethlehem together.

I was convinced that God had cursed me. I felt completely empty—like a water skin that has no water in it. No one could cheer me up or fill the hollowness inside of me.

I was so destitute that for a while I just lay around feeling sorry for myself. It was your mother who encouraged me to get up and try again. She knew that I felt like an enormous storm had ripped through my life and turned everything upside down. But she showed me the sun coming out after that terrible destruction. It was her selfless love that reminded me of God's faithfulness.

When I first stood up with Ruth at my side, I looked up at the sun breaking through the clouds and I thought about the God of our mothers and fathers. I remembered the many times that our people had lost hope and had been discouraged. I remembered that God always came through for them. And I asked for help. Then, I went for a long walk with God. I put my hand in his and shared everything with him. I told him how I felt that I had been abandoned, and I told him about how bitter I had become. Suddenly, I didn't feel so forsaken. Finally, I could accept that God was still there for me, that God wanted me to trust him completely. That was the day things started to change.

Not long after that, Ruth met your father, Boaz. He became our kinsman-redeemer. He bought the land my husband, Elimilech, had sold. And even though some people said Ruth was not one of us, he loved your mother and he married her. I believed that was the happiest day of my life. But I was wrong. The day you were born, I felt *completely* whole again. My life had worth and meaning again. My husband's and sons' name will live on.

Obed, my friends told me today that Ruth is better to me than seven sons, and they are right. To have seven sons means that a family is entirely complete. God used your mother to fill up my life and restore our family, Obed. I know that he will use you too. Listen to him speaking to you. Be a blessing to your people. Be a well that is full of cool, sweet water, where others may come to be refreshed.

Love,
Naomi

PRAYER

Thank you, Jesus, for being here, for holding my hand through this life. Lord, make me a channel of your peace. Where there is hatred let me bring your love. Help me to console, rather than be consoled. Fill me up with your spirit and your love. Amen.

FOLLOW-UP

Write down at least one promise that God has made to you. List the ways that God has kept that promise to you. Thank God for being faithful to you. Tuck the list away in your wallet. When you feel discouraged or empty, refer to it and remember and believe that your God will always keep the promises he has made.

our mother's voice

I n the tragic love story *Romeo and Juliet,* William Shakespeare wrote

What's in a name?
That which we call a rose,
By any other name would smell as sweet.

As you probably recall, Romeo could not be with his true love, Juliet, because his family and hers were archenemies. They had feuded for years. So even though Romeo and Juliet loved each other profoundly, marriage between the two was completely out of the question.

In this little speech, Romeo is musing about how different things might be if only Juliet had a different last name. She would still be the same sweet person, and his family's objections to her would disappear!

Names are an important part of our identity. They tell who we are; sometimes they even tell how we want people to see us. My daughter Jenny informed us shortly before leaving for university that she would be calling herself by her second name. She explained that it has a sweeter sound than her first given name. So it's not easy, but I'm trying hard to call her

Rosalynn instead of Jenny. I know her name is an important part of her identity.

Many of us have nicknames—names that carry warm, fuzzy feelings because they were given to us by an important someone. When that person calls us by that special name, we may feel especially loved or appreciated. Sometimes these people are the only ones who are allowed to call us by that familiar name. I will probably always think of my daughter as my Jenny Rose.

In today's society many women are choosing to contradict Shakespeare by using hyphenated surnames when they get married. They want to be identified by their own ancestry as well as by that of their spouse. Names matter. We have them, and we want others to use them correctly. When we affix our name to something, we say that it has importance and value.

Old Testament Jews, too, would have been happy to explain to Shakespeare that he was wrong. They believed a name was everything: it revealed your social and political status in the community. When a person's ancestry was recorded, the bloodline was traced through the males in the family. Men were known as "so and so, the son of the son of so and so." Jews traced their heritage to Abraham, the father of their race. There were twelve tribes, one for each of the sons of Jacob, the son of Abraham. To be of the tribe of Judah had special meaning and importance because that tribe would eventually produce the Messiah who had been promised to the Hebrew nation. This deliverer would free the Israelites from the oppression they suffered and would restore order and prosperity to the nation. To be part of that promise gave prominence, distinction, and status to a family.

In Matthew 1 the genealogy of Jesus is recorded for the Jews. Surprisingly, there are a few women's names among the men's: Tamar, the daughter-in-law of Judah, who tricked her father-in-law into sleeping with her; Rahab, the Canaanite prostitute, who protected Joshua's spies by hiding them in her house; and Ruth, the Moabite, the father of Obed, the grandfather of King David.

The names recorded in Matthew are the names of those who mattered, those who were important in the history of the nation. For two Gentile women to be included in this list has special significance. Especially because of their foreign background, these women could have no status, no name, no voice in their community. And yet Matthew gives them a place, a name, a voice in the genealogy of Jesus. They are the mothers of faith.

Ruth came to Bethlehem as a veiled, faceless stranger. She comes to us with a name fixed in the kingdom of God. She is a celebrity of faith who has a title, an identity in God's family.

Ruth has a second name too. It is the name of your mother, your sister, and your daughter. It is your name and my name. She is all of our voices. We can look in her eyes, listen to her story, and believe that we too have a face, a name, and a voice in the kingdom of God.

Shakespeare was right. It's not what we are called that matters. It's what we are.

PRAYER

Thank you, Jesus, that I may know you and call you by name. Thank you for the identity and the voice that you have given me. Teach me to live up to my name as a Christian. Help me to celebrate my life. Amen.

FOLLOW-UP

Look up the meaning of your name. Think about and decide on one way that you can "be" your name.

heads, hair, and sparrows

READ ESTHER 1:1-15 & LUKE 12:4-7.

Henry VIII would probably have cut off Queen Vashti's head if she were his wife. In Henry's day, royal wives who did not measure up were cut up. They were essentially defenseless victims who were easy prey to an all-powerful monarch.

Things have changed a lot since Henry's day. The descendant of this malicious king must struggle with his estranged spouse in a much more sophisticated way to try and cut her from his life. Princess Diana and Prince Charles of Britain are engaged in a tumultuous power struggle, using the media to play out their frustrations, their loneliness, their ambitions, and their need to be in control.

It would have been unimaginable to Xerxes, King of Persia, not to be able to dominate his wife. He would have understood Henry VIII much better than Prince Charles. He knew that women, including the wives of formidable monarchs, were subservient to their lords and masters: their husbands.

King Xerxes had given a magnificent three-month celebration. Everyone who was anyone in the one hundred and twenty-seven provinces of Persia was there. During this lavish festivity, the prominent leaders present were reminded of the incredible wealth that Persia had acquired. We can be quite certain that complimenting the king on his accomplishments and on the splendor and glory of his home and city was the thing to do.

The culmination of the commemoration was a banquet that lasted seven days. By the final day Xerxes was in "high spirits." That probably means that he was very drunk—feeling no pain. He decided that he wanted to display his beautiful queen to the gathering. He wanted to show her off as he had shown off all of his other possessions. This was a highly unusual thing for the king to do. Women in Xerxes' day were generally kept in seclusion; they were certainly never seen at public banquets.

Queen Vashti had been having her own party. When the eunuchs came to her with the king's command, she refused to obey. That response took incredible courage. Vashti literally put her life on the line by not coming to her husband. Obviously, there were strong-willed women even in the Persian Empire! Her husband was furious and "burned with anger."

There is no question that some people have legitimate authority over us and that we have an obligation to submit to that authority. But there are also instances when refusing to submit to an evil command is the right and honorable thing to do. You and I will never be caught in a power struggle of the magnitude of Xerxes and Vashti's; probably not even that of Charles and Diana's. However, especially as women, we will likely face situations in which control and might are factors. Despite the headway our culture has made to advance the rights of all people, there are still times when women are disempowered and intimidated.

There will probably always be some who want to exert control over others that they see as weaker or less capable. A bully in our society is not unlike Xerxes, who wanted to make sure that Vashti knew that he was the king and he was in charge. Those who are defenseless and vulnerable are easy targets for a tyrant who seeks to serve himself.

In spite of that, we don't have to be afraid. Every time a hair comes out of our head, God approves and knows about it. Every bird that nests in our trees, God knows and cares about. Whatever the hierarchy, God is the one who gives the authority, the one we must serve, and the one to whom we are accountable. That's absolute control!

When we stand before God one day, we will have to account to him—whatever our name or position. It will be clear to all of us, including the King of Persia, that God has always been in charge of history. For the Hebrew nation, and for you and me, that is the incredible significance of the story of Esther.

PRAYER

Thank you, Jesus, that you care about me and are in control of my life. Help me when I feel overwhelmed by the bullies in the world. Give me strength and courage when I must stand up for myself. Teach me to respect your authority. Amen.

FOLLOW-UP

Put up a bird feeder outside a window. As you watch the birds, remember that God takes care of each one of them. Take courage from the knowledge that God is in control of your life. He will take care of you, no matter what or who happens in your life.

a fashion statement

READ ESTHER 1:16-22 & EPHESIANS 6:10-18.

Are you old enough to remember Twiggy? What about Doris Day, Marilyn Monroe, or Madonna? Fortunately these are only a few of the many female superstars who have influenced women in the last few decades. Women such as Mother Theresa and Margaret Thatcher have also presented interesting new prototypes of what a modern woman can be.

People who are in the spotlight often present an impression to the world about how to look and how to act. Through the way they dress and behave, values and attitudes—not only about fashion, but also about life—are conveyed. And others are quick to imitate them.

The more things change, the more they stay the same. Interestingly enough, about four hundred years before Christ even the mighty Persian Empire looked to its superstar, its queen, for direction on conduct and demeanor. That fact prompted quick action by Xerxes when his wife defied him. If the wives of nobles heard about the queen's disregard for her husband's wishes, they might very well behave in the same despicable way. This would not look very good for Xerxes, especially when he had just spent three months bragging about how magnificent he was. No matter what he thought of his wife, he had to act; he had to save face in front of his prestigious nobles and officials. He had to show that he was the all-powerful sovereign.

The prominent leaders of the Persia Empire sat on the edge of their seats as Queen Vashti's fate was decided. Her crime was definitely a felony. But unlike sensational lawbreakers of our day, Queen Vashti did not get her day in court. She was presumed to be guilty as charged. The eyes of the Persian Empire's leaders were fixed on her as her fate was decided. With her refusal to come at the king's command, she had transgressed against all of the men in the empire.

A queen in the Persian Empire had some very specific responsibilities. Among the most important were to obey the king and to produce an heir for him. We aren't told whether Vashti had a son, although historians believe that it was her son who became the king after

Xerxes died. Perhaps that is the reason she was allowed to live. Her retribution was that she would never again be allowed in her husband's presence. She would be replaced as the number one wife. Vashti was out, someone new would be in.

Vashti must have been a pretty spunky lady. It took a lot of daring to do what she did. We don't know what her motives were for refusing to come to the king. If she was trying to set a new trend for women, she was unsuccessful. I have the feeling she didn't accomplish what she wanted. The axe that severed her from the king's life also amputated her status and authority in the realm. As the queen, Vashti obviously had a responsibility to set an example for women in her society.

We may have difficulty understanding or accepting the norms and customs of the day, but we can certainly understand that there were expectations for her to live up to. Women today also face many demands. Often we have more than one role to perform. There may be times we pattern our service on others that we respect and admire. Who we choose as mentors and models for our life will definitely impact who we are. Obviously, we have many more options than the women of the Persian Empire did. But that also makes us more accountable and responsible.

We need to make important decisions about the lifestyle and attitudes that we dress ourselves in. It may be tempting and daring to browse through the shopping malls of the world. There are many celebrated faces and names that can be tried on. And there is a convenient return policy. Products can be worn and exchanged if they don't fit. The selection is colorful and dazzling.

But there is another option. We can choose to wear the armor of God described in Ephesians 6. It will fit perfectly, will never wear out or need to be replaced. And it will definitely make a fashion statement.

PRAYER

Thank you, Jesus, for the women and men who model Christian values in the world. Thank you for the model of how to dress in your Word. Help me to boldly wear your armor. Teach me to be a Christian fashion statement. Amen.

FOLLOW-UP

Write a letter to person who has exemplified the Christian lifestyle for you. Tell the person how important and meaningful her/his witness has been for you. Thank God for that person.

chosen

READ ESTHER 2:1-7 & PSALM 139:13-18.

I can remember a time in my life when dates were dried-up prunes and parties were more than one family on a telephone line. The anxiety of not being wanted ruled my existence. Sometimes it took me by the neck and choked me so I couldn't speak. It put me on a leash and led me places that I didn't want to go. It pried my mouth open and put things in it that I didn't want there. It turned on a boom box in my head and made words come out of my mouth that weren't mine. My teenage years were a desperate, lonely time in which I knew everything and nothing all at once.

The girls who were examined as possibilities for the future queen of Persia were likely gripped by the same kind of apprehension. What had happened to Vashti was common knowledge. The same thing could happen to any woman who belonged to the king.

Being the queen of Persia was not always as attractive as it appeared. The king had lots of wives. They were well looked after. There were servants, beautiful clothes, and lots of luxuries. However, there was also a good chance that a girl would spend only one night of her life with her husband. If she didn't please him, she might never see him again. That didn't mean she could go home to her family and friends and marry her sweetheart. She had to spend the rest of her life sequestered in the sultry, constrained quarters of the harem. She would never mother a child, and she would probably have few friends. The harem was often a detached, lonely place. Discouragement about being neglected by the king didn't always bring out the best in wives.

Nevertheless there was considerable fanfare as the king's entourage entered a village. All of the teenage girls were lined up and closely examined. Some would be quickly rejected because they weren't exquisite enough. Others would be inspected more than once. Some would be selected to go to the citadel at Susa to be groomed for the king's harem. Imagine the trepidation that each girl must have felt, waiting, wondering if she would be chosen.

Esther stood in one of those lines of young women. She knew that being chosen would make life very unusual and difficult. She would be forced to participate in many activities that were contrary to the good Jewish upbringing Mordecai, her uncle, had given her. (I wonder if her fear of being chosen was similar to my fear of being rejected.)

Esther was a stunningly beautiful young woman. She carried herself with dignity, but she was not proud or haughty. She knew how to talk and how to behave. She said all the proper and polite things at the appropriate times. If I had been a teenager standing next to Esther, I would have envied her grace and charm. I would have coveted her popularity. I would have understood why she was chosen, but I would have resented it.

The jealousy we may feel when someone is more popular and better liked than we are is probably understandable, especially when we are teens. Rejection or the fear of it can have a tremendous influence on who we are. It can shape our personalities. That's probably because the need to be loved is a basic human requirement: People were created for each other.

I think that's why God tells us that he has chosen us before we were even born. God knew us and accepted us before we even knew ourselves. We don't have to stand in a line and be examined like Esther was to see if we are good enough. We don't have to be controlled by the kind of phobia that infested my life. God already knows us and welcomes us. He knit us together in our mother's womb. No matter how repulsive we perceive ourselves to be, God wants us and selects us.

Although there is no beauty contest to win, there is a crown to be had. Imagine how wonderful it will fit for all eternity!

PRAYER

Lord, thank you for choosing me. Help me to let go of my fears. Help me to know and believe that you want me. Teach me to live my life completely with that knowledge. Amen.

FOLLOW-UP

Cut out a shiny crown and put it on your fridge. When you look at it, remember that you are chosen and that a real crown is waiting for you.

stay away from the water

The reality of death came to life in the quiet of the room. Two nine-year-old girls stood alone, clutching each other. As they smelled the sweet stench of the flowers and looked at their lifeless friend lying in a white satin box, for the first time in their lives death was more than a word.

It had been a beautiful, picture-perfect summer's day at the beach—a day filled with laughter, splashing, sand castles, games, and blown-up inner tubes in the water. Of course, there were mothers too, with reminders: "Don't go too far out. Remember there's an undertow."

The children knew the words. But not until the water snatched a friend that day did they understand the meaning. The memory of that day and all the fear and sorrow it brought with it is etched into my mind and heart.

Many years later the fear of water and its power cut deeper when my dear father-in-law drowned in a boating accident. So when my children were born, I was determined to protect them and myself from the dangers of the water.

That wasn't always easy. When my children were young, our family often walked over a small footbridge to the park. It had no sides, so I was constantly fearful that my children would peer over the edge and fall in. As they grew older, my worry extended past the footbridge to other circumstances. Whenever they left home, my parting words would be the same: "Have fun, be safe, and stay away from the water." Sometimes those words must have sounded silly. I knew the kids were going camping by a lake and that they'd be swimming and boating. But I'd say it anyway.

Over the years, "stay away from the water" took on new meaning in my family. When my children and I talked about "staying away from the water," we meant avoiding situations that were not safe. After all, if you "stay away from the water," you can't drown in it.

When Esther moved to the palace, she became part of a world filled with danger, competition, pleasure, and luxury. People in and around the harem were willing to do almost anything to gain power and control. Esther could easily have become involved in the plotting and scheming that went on to become the king's chosen one. Everybody at the palace liked Esther. In fact, she became a favorite of the eunuch Hegai, who was in charge. It would have been so easy for her to forget who she was and jump into the waters and have a good time.

But as a child, Esther had learned from Mordecai that a good Jew follows many customs and rules—and "stays away from the water." While at the palace, she communicated regularly with Mordecai. She continued to listen to and follow his instruction even though she was fully involved in the life at the harem. Her training as a child enabled her to keep her feet planted on solid ground.

Our world is not that much different from Esther's. The temptations that surrounded her also surround us. All around us are people who don't know or care who we are or what we stand for. Sometimes it's tempting to go for a little swim, just to see how the water feels.

We don't really know a lot about how Esther managed to stay away from the water. We do know that she was reminded and encouraged by her family.

We need to remind and encourage each other too. That's why I taught my children to stay away from the water. I also taught them how to swim when the water is impossible to avoid.

PRAYER

Lord, thank you for the people in my life who care about me. Help me to appreciate their love and to listen to them. Give me the strength to stay away from the water. Amen.

FOLLOW-UP

Tell at least one person who loves you that you appreciate his/her help in staying away from the water.

wearing the identity

READ ESTHER 2:10, 19-20 & MATTHEW 26:69-75.

The distinctive black habit of the Ursiline Sisters fascinated me as a child. I didn't understand, at that time, the significance of the long black robes with their starched, stiff wimples. But I did know what these women were about: the large crucifix that hung around their necks made it very clear to me that these were people who had committed their lives to the Lord. They were Christians. I envied their boldness in making this declaration.

In our society, people often wear uniforms that help others recognize their roles. Police officers and fire fighters are a few professionals that are easy to identify because of the clothing they wear. When we see these people, we have certain expectations for them. We assume that a police officer can be trusted to help us if we are in trouble. A fire fighter will go into a burning home to rescue someone.

Using clothing and symbols to identify people is not a new idea. Already in Esther's day, people were recognized and identifed by the clothing they wore. Jews who didn't want their neighbors to identify them as Hebrews simply avoided wearing the traditional Jewish dress.

Mordecai was one of those who didn't wear the "star of David" prominently on his clothing. And he warned Esther to avoid telling others about her nationality and family background too.

Historians tell us that there was a long history of conflict between the Jews and the Amalekites, who also lived in Persia. Even though the Jews had been given the freedom to return to Israel, many had chosen to remain in Persia and had assumed important business positions in the country. But because of the hostility between these two nations of people, the Jews who had remained behind often tried to blend in with the Amalekites. That's what Mordecai warned Esther to do: "Don't let them know you're a Jew!" he said. He must have known that some people would be opposed to having a Jewish girl as the queen of Persia.

So no one knew Esther was a Jew. We aren't told how she kept it a secret, but we do know that it must have been very difficult for her to follow all the customs, rules, and rituals that

God required of the Jewish people without letting anyone catch on.

Any of us who have tried a similar deception understand how complicated it can be. Keeping our religious identity neatly wrapped under our clothes can be tempting at times, but it is also very difficult. There are certainly occasions when it's much simpler just to pretend that we're part of the crowd and do what everyone else does. Then we don't have to worry about being different or about standing out. We can try to tell ourselves that we can be Christlike without anyone knowing; we can practice what we believe behind closed doors. But eventually it didn't work for Esther—or for Peter. It's not likely to work for us either.

The Ursiline Sisters have made considerable changes in their style of dress since I was a child. But they're still committed to openly wearing their identity. I pray that you and I may be graced with the same faithfulness.

PRAYER

Thank you, Jesus, for calling me to wear your name. Give me the courage and the grace to do so boldly. Help me in my words and actions to show that I belong to you. Help me to name you publicly. Amen.

FOLLOW-UP

In a meaningful way tell at least one person (who doesn't already know) about your commitment as a Christian.

b e a u t y

READ ESTHER 2:12-18 & SONG OF SONGS 4:1-15.

The magnificent maple in my backyard stands stripped, completely naked, arms outstretched and waiting. I can almost hear its limbs groaning with the cold of winter, the splendor of its summer foliage long forgotten.

Some will argue that the tree is at its most beautiful standing there exposed, that it shows vigor and strength in its waiting for the renewal of life and its true self. Others find more beauty in the simplicity, freshness, and growth of spring buds. Still others prefer the lavishness of summer greens or the magnificence of autumn's colorful palette. Beauty is, after all, in the eye of the beholder.

In our world beauty is a multibillion-dollar industry. Advertisements encourage us to believe that being attractive is a necessary component for being happy and successful. They tell us which clothes, makeup, deodorant, perfume, and other accessories will make us desirable to others: if you wear the right stockings, everyone will think your legs are beautiful. If you wear the right scent, the man or woman of your dreams will fall in love with you. Even though we mock many of these ads, most of us are more influenced by the "quest for beauty" than we would like to admit.

Esther knew about the pressure to be beautiful too. Imagine what these young women went through during the twelve months that they prepared to meet King Xerxes. The king's eunuchs trained, pampered, and coached these young women to please the king in every imaginable way. A whole year of the right food, massages, mud baths, and relaxation, with the sole purpose of being beautiful. Making a good first impression was very important if you wanted to be remembered by the king.

Esther succeeded at this full-time vocation of looking beautiful—she was the winner. But what about the girls who didn't cut it? How disappointing it must have been when they were told they weren't attractive enough for the king. For a year these young women had made beauty their only focus, their sole hope for the future. To them, not being beautiful enough must have seemed catastrophic. (Unfortunately, that thinking is alive and well in today's society!)

Of all the beautiful girls, Esther was picked to be queen. We are told that she pleased the king in every way and was popular with everyone in the harem. What made Esther stand out from the others? Perhaps it was her simplicity. She was told that when she went to the king, she could take anything with her that she wanted—some special gown, jewels, anything that might make her more attractive. She chose to take nothing.

There is no question that Esther was an exquisite, stunning young lady. But it took more than outer beauty for her to make the impression she did. Her inner character and her love for God flowed through every part of her being, making her "beauty" stand out.

That's an important point for us to remember in a society that places so much value on outward appearances. My maple tree helps remind me that without the lifeblood that flows through the tree, without the trunk that holds it up through the cold long winter, without the roots that feed it and support it, the tree would be just a heap of dead wood. In whatever season or expression we see beauty, there must be life and essence on the inside to make the loveliness vital and meaningful on the outside.

PRAYER

Jesus, thank you for loving and accepting me, for making me beautiful in your image. Help me to learn what looking good as your child means and to know what your image is for me. Teach me to appreciate the diversity of beauty in people and in your world. Thank you for the gift of beauty. Amen.

FOLLOW-UP

Identify something beautiful about yourself. Think about why this quality makes you beautiful. Tell someone you love what you think is beautiful about them. Talk about the essence of beauty with that person.

have you heard God whisper?

READ ESTHER 2:19-23 & JUDGES 4.

"I heard the call to give up all and follow Christ into the slums to serve him among the poorest of the poor."

Do you recognize the quote? Mother Theresa, the woman who said those words, is acknowledged worldwide as a modern-day saint. When Theresa first heard God's call, she willingly gave up a comfortable teaching job in a rich school in India to begin her work among that country's poor—the "untouchables" whom everyone else had discarded. Her commitment and courage have earned her the prestigious Nobel Peace Prize and an honorable place in world history.

Mother Theresa didn't set out to make a name for herself. All she did was simply and honestly obey God's call, ignoring all those who tried to dissuade her. Her example has made her a powerful witness. As Indira Ghandi, former Prime Minister of India, noted, "She lives the truth that prayer is devotion, prayer is service. Service is her concern, her religion, her redemption. To meet her is to feel utterly hum-ble, to sense the power of tenderness, the strength of love."

Like Mother Theresa, Esther heard and followed God's call. It came in the voice of Mordecai, Esther's cousin and guardian. Esther could have made herself undesirable and therefore ineffective at the court of King Xerxes. Instead, she kept her eyes and ears open, waiting for opportunities. When Mordecai told her of the plot against the king, she was in a position to save his life. Later there would be other demands.

In his book *Daughters Who Dared* Gerald Zandstra tells of women who, like Mother Theresa and Esther, answered God's call. The stories of Johanna Veenstra, Henrietta Bierenga, Nella Breen, and several others, women who were pioneers on a mission field in Africa, are wonderful reminders that the courage and conviction of ordinary, simple women can make a difference. Faced with seemingly insurmountable barriers, these women courageously answered God's call—a call that came in the voice of a country and a people in need.

In the Bible, too, we read of women who listened and answered the call. Miriam, Deborah, Ruth, Anna, and Mary are just a few. To understand how important these women are, remember that in the Jewish culture women did not have the standing they do today. A woman's main purpose in life was to have children and carry on her husband's name. The stories of Esther and others like her must have been especially motivating for women who had little or no rank in the social order.

Hearing and following God's call can be very complicated for women today too—in some ways even more complicated than it was in Esther's day. While we may not agree with the cultural customs and norms of the Jewish people, it seems safe to say that the women of the Old Testament knew what was expected of them. The church, society, and family pretty much agreed what a woman's role was.

That's just not so in our society today. The church, society, and family all still hold firm ideas about the place and role of women. But often those ideas clash or conflict. Sometimes the noise and confusion created by the pandemonium of uncertainties may make it very difficult to listen and to hear God calling. It may make knowing what God wants from us very complex.

As you read and think about Esther, listen for God's message to you. We are all called to serve. What that service will be for you and me is ultimately between God and us. Other may help us to understand and even fulfill our calling, but we must work hard ourselves to know what is expected of us. It may be a simple task or it may be a challenge filled with doubt and confusion. Reading the stories of women who have courageously heard and answered the call can encourage and support us.

Esther, Mother Theresa, Johanna Veenstra, and you and I worship the same God. Whether it comes in the plea of a friend, the cry of child, the groaning of a nation, or the whispered voice of God, we must hear and respond to God's call.

PRAYER

Thank you for calling me to serve you. Give me the desire to study your Word and help me to know your will for my life. Speak loudly, Lord, and help me to tune out the noise in my life so that I can hear what you are saying. Give me the courage to hear and answer your call. Amen.

FOLLOW-UP

Identify one person you admire who has clearly answered God's call. Find out how that person has heard the call to serve. Make a list of what you can learn from the person.

reflections in the mirror

READ ESTHER 3:1-4 & JAMES 1:22-27.

Look in the mirror. Who looks back at you? Is it the child you used to be? The person you will become? Or do you see the person you are right now, today? What's in the eyes of the person who looks back at you? Do you like her? Are you proud of her? Do you like to spend time with her?

Mordecai sat at the city gate watching and listening. To have a place there he must have been important in the civil service of the Persian Empire. He had influence, position. Four years had passed since he had saved the king's life. Strangely, he had received no recognition for this action.

In contrast, Haman, the king's right-hand man, was rewarded richly and openly for his service to the king. He was promoted to such a prominent position that all nobles were ordered to bow down to him. Mordecai could have and should have given Haman the respect he was entitled to by law, but he refused. Maybe he finally looked into the mirror of his life and didn't like what he saw.

By this time Mordecai had revealed his identity as a Jew. We don't know what caused him

to divulge this secret. He might just have had enough of being pushed around by a bully like Haman. Or he might have looked at himself and saw a man who didn't look or act like a Jew. The *NIV Study Bible* explains that Haman was probably an Amalekite. There was a long history of friction between the Jews and the Amalekites. Perhaps Haman's arrogance and his ancestry were just enough to make Mordecai realize that he had to take a stand and be himself. He was a Jew, and he would not bow down to Haman, the Amalekite.

We also aren't told what made Mordecai so openly defiant. He must have known that there would be consequences to his actions. Haman was a very powerful man. Mordecai was astute enough to know about the ruthless conspiracies that were a regular part of life at the king's court. It seems strange that he didn't consider what might happen to him or to Esther as a result of such blatant contempt for Haman. If Haman reacted, as Mordecai must have known he would, who would take his place in watching over Esther? He loved her as his own daughter. Surely he didn't want to jeopardize her life.

Nevertheless, Mordecai sat at the city gate and refused to obey the law. Whatever his reasons, he could not endure Haman's behavior.

We too may be faced with intolerable behavior from time to time. Do we bow with the acceptance of silence when someone mocks the God we believe in? Do we sit mutely offended and angry as a racist or sexist joke is told? To stand up and speak out in such situations takes some of the boldness that Mordecai displayed. There is, of course, the possibility that we will make a spectacle of ourselves, that we will be singled out or scorned as Mordecai was. We may have to pay dearly for our actions.

Mordecai made a difficult decision based on who he was. He was no longer willing to hide the fact that he was a Jew. It was time to act on his convictions.

All of us come to decision points in our lives—times when we need to embrace what we believe and who we are. Learning about ourselves is not an easy or quick process. It takes more than just looking in the bathroom mirror. James tells us that we can use the "perfect law" as a mirror for our lives. That law will give us the freedom, the insight, the strength and the courage to be the Christians we are called to be.

When you and I meet the person in the mirror, we need to remember that because we are loved by God, we need to love and respect ourselves. We can be confident that God will empower us to be the persons he wants us to be. Then we will be able to sit at the city gates of our lives and face ourselves, face the people we encounter there, and face the results of our actions.

PRAYER

Thank you, Jesus, for mirrors to look into. Help me to use your Word as the ultimate mirror for my life. Give me the courage and strength to be honest about myself and my actions. Give me the grace to face who I am and to act as myself. Forgive me when I fall short. Amen.

FOLLOW-UP

Look at yourself in the mirror. Write a letter to yourself, answering as many of the questions at the beginning of the devotion as you can. Ask some new questions about yourself, too, and try to answer them during the next few weeks.

hearing the bell

READ ESTHER 3:5-15 & JOHN 15:18-27.

It rose ominously twelve feet in the air. The forbidding barrier of twenty-six-and-a-half miles of concrete and barbed wire was called the "Wall of Shame" by West Berliners. It isolated and segregated families, streets, beliefs, and even graveyards. The wall's smooth, cold, concrete sides and threatening rolls of thorny wire made it unscalable. Those who tried were quickly riveted with bullets that plunged them to a certain death.

In 1993, when I stood and touched the rigid, calloused exterior of a piece of that wall that had once divided a city, I shuddered. I knew I couldn't come close to imagining the extent of the atrocities caused by this foreboding slab of stone.

In the same way it is impossible for us to imagine what the decree from Xerxes meant to the Jews living in the Persian Empire. The signs were posted in every province and in every language. On the twelfth day of the twelfth month, all Jews—young, old, men, women, and children—would be slaughtered. Their property would be plundered, taken by their murderers. There was no place to hide, nowhere to run.

People must have been very confused. Why was Xerxes doing this heinous thing? What had caused the king to issue a decree that would inflict such anguish? What kind of a ruler could perpetrate such a monstrosity?

During World War II the same questions were asked about Hitler, a modern-day Xerxes. Only those who suffered under his Reich will truly be able to appreciate the horrifying terror that must have swept across the land.

The person behind the edict, of course, was Haman. Mordecai had really incensed Haman. He was frothing at the mouth. The fact that Mordecai refused to give him the reverence he thought he deserved enraged Haman. It is hard to believe that his animosity could be so extreme that he would go to such lengths to get even—that he would plan the destruction of a whole nation of people. But he did.

Unfortunately, the kind of hatred that controlled Hamen is alive and well in the 1990s. I'm sure we could all tell a personal story of tyranny and oppression. These tales of cruelty can leave us feeling discouraged and disheartened. They bring the reality of the persecution of God's people very close to home.

Jesus frankly tells us that as his followers we must expect the world to hate us in the same way it hated him. I find this an unpleasant thought. What makes it bearable is knowing that Christ overcame being nailed to a cross. He broke the Satanic chains that had tried to hold the human race ransom.

The forces of evil have great strength and intensity. They can construct solid, powerful walls. Walls that can entomb virtue and goodness in concrete and barbed wire. Walls that can kill and destroy our bodies. Walls that will try to ravage our very souls.

But because of Christ's victory near the walls, we often find symbols of hope. Every day in the town hall of the city of West Berlin, a bell rang out loudly and clearly across the city and across the wall. The Bell of Freedom reminded Berliners of the hope that their city would be reunited. It reminded them to keep the faith and not be discouraged by the seemingly impenetrable restraints of evil that held them in its clutches.

When I touched a piece of the broken-down Berlin Wall, I could hear the bell ringing. The hard concrete reminded me that there would always be pieces of the wall for me to feel and view. Pieces that I must keep working at breaking down. The pealing of the bell in my head assured me that wherever a Berlin Wall or a Haman rises up, there will be a clanging cymbal of hope.

For the Jews in Persia, that bell was a covenant with an omnipotent God. It would ring loudly and clearly for them. It also rings for you and me.

I thank God that I can hear the bell ringing.

PRAYER

Thank you, Jesus, for the bells that remind me of the hope and love that you have for me. Give me the strength to deal with the walls of oppression that the world builds. Help me to ring out strong and true for you. Amen.

FOLLOW-UP

Identify someone who is suffering because of a wall or a Haman. In some small way sound a bell of hope for the person. Send a card, make a visit, extend your hand of friendship as a symbol of hope.

the right place,
the right time

READ ESTHER 4:1-14 & PSALM 33.

Dear Esther,
 I wish that I could come and hold you and rock you in my arms the way that I used to when you were a little girl. Hathach, your eunuch, has told me how confused and troubled you are. When he realized that I am a Jew, I think he understood why you have been in so much agony. It didn't take too much thinking to figure out where you fit in.

He loves you and was shocked that you would be killed along with the rest of us. I tried to explain to him that God will save us, but I know he thinks that I'm deluding myself. He just doesn't understand that our God is stronger and more powerful than Xerxes or any of his laws. But I know that you believe this, Esther, and that is why I am writing you this letter.

I have returned the clothes you sent. I can't take off my sackcloth until I have some idea of what God wants us to do. Esther, you saw and read the edict that Xerxes has published. You must know by now how grave this situation is. We have all been sentenced to death. You are included in this sentence, Esther; you won't be

able to hide. Haman has spies everywhere, and it won't be long before someone figures out the connection between you and me. They will know you are one of us, and you won't be able to escape. Haman's butchers will see to that.

All the Jews in the city are in a state of shock. Even those who have never acknowledged their heritage know that it is only a matter of time before someone finds out they are Jews. Many think that all appears to be lost. It's the same everywhere in the empire. I have seen mothers rocking their babies, stunned into complete silence because they don't know where to turn for help. The young children are the most pathetic; they know something is terribly wrong, but they don't have any understanding of what it's all about. No one can explain it to them or comfort them.

Esther, I have thought and prayed much about what we need to do. Before I tell you what it is, I want you to think about the stories you learned when you were a little girl. I remember that you loved to hear the story of Joseph. I think you felt sorry for him because he was punished for things he hadn't done. Our people are just like that now as we prepare to bear the brunt of Haman's anger. He is obsessed by his hatred of Jews. In spite of the way things look, I know there is an answer, and I believe you are part of it. You must help our people, Esther!

Remember how Joseph was in the right place at the right time to save his family? You are in the same place as he was, Esther! Think about all the times you asked me why God would want you to be the queen of Persia. I believe God put you there for this time and this purpose. You are in a position to do something about the terrible fate we face. You must believe that you have a decisive place in God's plan.

I know that going to your husband and asking for help is a terrifying thought. But I believe that you are one of the few people he really cares about. He will listen to you. Xerxes will be getting a lot of money from Haman for allowing him to go ahead with this despicable deal. But I don't think money really means much to him; he's rich enough. You mean more than money to Xerxes. He chose you over all those other women, and I think he loves you. He knows you are different, and I'm sure he doesn't want to lose you. You have to try to persuade him to save not only your life but the lives of your people.

Esther, you must remember that we are the chosen people of God. It is from us that a Messiah will come to restore order and peace in the world. I know this will happen with or without your help. God has been with you at the palace. He has taken care of you and given you people who love you and have supported you. Our God won't let you down now. But you have to trust God now the way you trusted me when you were a little girl. God has given you a prominent place and has made you strong. Now you must act as his child. Put your hand in God's and let him guide you and protect you as you decide what you must do.

Love,
Mordecai

PRAYER

Thank you that I am your child. Thank you for people who encourage me to know your will for my life. Help me to know what my place is in your kingdom. Give me the courage to make difficult choices and to act on those decisions. Amen.

FOLLOW-UP

Write a letter of thanks to someone who has helped you make difficult life choices. Thank God for the support and encouragement the person gives you.

holding hands

READ ESTHER 4:15-17 & PSALM 5.

My Dear Uncle Mordecai,
     A dark, ominous shroud has been cast over my existence. The fear that has filled my heart has been like the obscure emptiness of an unlit street. In this void, I haven't known where to turn. I have tried to escape into the doors of selfishness and denial, but I have found no haven there. The bandits of greed have been around me, threatening to pounce and take what is left of me. In this emptiness there has been no one to trust. When you weren't there to reassure me, the relentless wailing from the city penetrated my confidence and left me feeling abandoned and lifeless.

Your letter appeared as a light in the window. It gave me direction. How good it feels to know that I will be able to cast off the disguise that has been masking my existence!

Mordecai, you know that I took your advice about keeping who I am a secret. But now I feel a great sense of relief. The camouflage I have been wearing has been heavy and often very uncomfortable. What lies ahead terrifies me. But this new fear is different because I know that there is hope for us to survive.

In many ways life has been so comfortable for me here that this is the first time I have really thought about it ending. Now that we can hear the Jews in the streets crying, we are very careful about what we say and do; no one wants to be reported as being disloyal and risk the wrath of Xerxes. Some women are complaining about the noise they have to put up with. It's all I can do not to scream at them to stop their complaining. The law Xerxes has made to kill all Jews is making everyone really nervous. They're all wondering who will be next on Haman's hit list.

Mordecai, I have thought a lot about dying. In fact, I can't seem to think of anything else. Your letter made me realize that I can't just sit here any longer and do nothing. You were right about Haman finding out who I am. Sometimes I hear the eunuchs whispering about me, and I always wonder if they know the truth. Most of them are very kind and seem to care about me, but still it has been very hard to carry this secret around. I have decided that I don't want to die and I don't want my people to be destroyed either. If I must die, I will do it trying to make a difference.

So I am going to talk to Xerxes. Mordecai, this is going to be dangerous because he hasn't asked for me in the last thirty days. He has called for other wives instead of me—so I'm wondering if he has grown tired of me already. I know this often happens with him; some women only see him once in their whole lifetime. I will have to go and request an audience with him in the inner court. The law says that anyone who enters there will be killed unless Xerxes extends his gold scepter to the person. I know that I must do as you said, Mordecai, and put my hand in God's. Only God can protect me from the anger of the king. But I'm really scared, Mordecai!

Please pray for me often in the next few days. My heart thunders and my hands tremble as I think about going to talk to my husband. I'll do what I can to prepare myself. My maids and I will be fasting and praying for three days and nights. But I need your help and the help of other Jews in Susa too. Please ask all of them to pray for me. We must take hold of God's promise to protect us, his people. I know that only God can remove the shroud that threatens to cover us all.

Mordecai, I have never told you how much you mean to me. Now that it looks as if we may all die, know that I love you. You have been a wonderful father to me. You have always been there for me and supported me. Please do so again.

I know now that I am not alone. Pray that God will give me courage and keep me safe.

Love,
Esther

PRAYER

Thank you, Jesus, that I never need to feel alone. Thank you for holding me in the palm of your hand. Help me when I must walk dark, lonely streets to put my hand in yours. Teach me to trust you completely. Amen.

FOLLOW-UP

Put a marble in your change purse. When you feel alone or frightened, hold it in the palm of your hand and know that God holds you there and keeps you safe. Share the knowledge with a friend.

near to the heart of God

READ ESTHER 4:15-16 & PSALM 19.

The kiss of the sun for pardon,
The song of the birds for mirth—
One is nearer God's heart in the garden
Than anywhere else on earth.

This song by St. Francis of Assisi is inscribed on a plaque in my garden. In spring, when the first crocus blooms and the earth are waking up again, I understand what St. Francis meant. Spring and summer are times to celebrate life, times to work in the flower beds or walk on a quiet country road. These beautiful places are full of some of God's best handiwork, and it is here that I feel near to the heart of God.

When Esther needed to find courage and strength to approach the king, she drew near to the heart of God too. She went into seclusion with her servants to fast and to pray. Esther spent three days and nights strengthening and preparing herself for the task God had given her to do.

In our fast-paced world, time is a very precious commodity. Few of us would ever consider praying and meditating for three days—no matter what crisis we faced. And it's true that Esther probably had much more time to herself than we do. She didn't have to worry about looking after a sick, crying baby, going to work, getting dinner ready, doing the laundry, or getting the kids to their piano lessons on time.

In spite of that, when I think about her awesome responsibility of risking her life to save her people, I don't think I'd want to change places with her. She teaches me something important about how to prepare to face whatever lies before me. Esther knew that she had to ready herself in mind and in body to approach the king. The time she would spend with God would fortify her for the task.

Fasting is no longer a common practice or means of worship. However, the need to find places and ways to be in touch with God and our own feelings is as important for us as it was for Esther. We must all find our own quiet, alone, safe places to renew ourselves, places that we can communicate with God, places to prepare ourselves for the challenges of our everyday lives.

For me that place is my garden. As I admire the colors or the incredible uniqueness of a single flower, I remember and praise God for the beauty in nature and in my life. When I see the intricate patterns of a butterfly, I am reminded of how fragile life is and how it must be appreciated. While digging in the dirt, I am able to think, pray, and reflect in God's presence. Sometimes the problems and concerns of the day are spilled out and I am able to bury them in the dirt. Like a bad weed, they may come back, but their roots will be weaker, and I will be able to deal with them again.

Esther spent three days and nights praying and fasting to receive strength and courage from God. We too must find quiet, safe places where we can be near to the heart of God. We must commit to talking and listening to God if we want to know our Creator's will for our lives. Then, like Esther, we will be equipped and available to face whatever challenge the world may throw at us.

PRAYER

Thank you, Lord, for revealing yourself in your Word and in your world. Thank you for the beauty in nature; help me to see and know your greatness there. Encourage me with your Spirit to spend time with you away from the noise and clutter of life. Strengthen and support me in my effort to serve you. Amen.

FOLLOW-UP

Think of a safe, quiet place where you can be alone with God. Make a commitment to spend a specific amount of time there each day to be near to the heart of God.

dinner with the lions

READ ESTHER 5:1-8 & DANIEL 6:13-23.

She stood tall and regal, her head held high. Her face was much more than beautiful. It seemed to radiate a serene, confident attractiveness. Her smile was gracious and warm. An elegant gown of deep, purple satin flowed from her shoulders to the floor in rich, soft layers. A train of a deeper hue was draped from her shoulders and trailed on the floor. Her hand was raised and touched an ornate, gold scepter. She was the portrait of a queen—elegant, majestic, and dignified.

That's how I remember a picture that hung on the wall in my Sunday school classroom many years ago. It was an artist's concept of Queen Esther approaching King Xerxes. The portrayal was one of several in a collection of Bible illustrations. They were held together on the top and had to be flipped over each week. I don't remember any of the other people in the collection. But, in my mind's eye, I can still clearly, vividly see Esther standing there looking so magnificent. To me, she exemplified how a beautiful, Christian woman would look and act under pressure.

As Esther slowly, majestically walked from her quarters to the king's hall, the tension must have been incredible. Everyone at the palace knew the risk she was taking. There must have been hushed whispering in the corridors behind the lavish tapestries that covered the doorways. Esther was liked and respected by everyone in the palace. Some of her friends must have wondered in silent trepidation why she would be risking her life to talk to Xerxes.

As the court watched and held its breath, Esther approached the king. I think as she stood before him, she must have looked much like the woman in that long-ago Sunday school picture. Xerxes was sitting on his throne facing the door. Struck by her regal beauty, he immediately held out his royal scepter to spare her life. In fact, he was so impressed that he offered her anything she wanted—up to half of his kingdom.

Imagine how amazed people must have been as Esther invited Xerxes and Haman for dinner. Why would she risk everything to ask them to a banquet? What was so important that it needed to be talked about in private? Of course, what they didn't realize was that Esther had prepared herself for this meeting. She had planned and thought out her actions prayerfully and carefully. She had ventured willingly into the lion's den, knowing that she could be pounced on and destroyed by a pack of hungry beasts.

Later in the Old Testament, Daniel stood up to another Persian king by physically standing in a lion's den. The amazement his friends felt when they discovered he was not harmed must have been the same kind of relief that Esther's friends felt when she was spared by Xerxes.

When Xerxes and Haman came to dinner, Xerxes repeated his offer to Esther about granting her wish. And again she said, "I'd like you to come for dinner again tomorrow night." Xerxes and Haman must have been curious about these unusual requests. They must have wondered what Esther really wanted.

Again, it might have appeared to onlookers that Esther was taking an unnecessary risk by not getting to the point. But the young queen showed amazing courage and grace and didn't seem to be apprehensive about what she was doing.

Our society does not have the kind of laws that subject us to the risks that Esther and Daniel had to endure. But there are still places where anger, greed, or hate can threaten to devour us—places where sinister, lion-like beasts may be waiting to pounce on us and consume us. When we venture into places that are unfriendly to our Christianity, we may feel like we are in a virtual lion's den.

Sometimes it may be tempting to behave like a lion when we are in its presence. If Esther had come into the king's hall ranting and raving like an angry lion, protesting that his laws weren't fair, she probably wouldn't have lived till dinner time.

If we put ourselves in the portrait of Queen Esther, we can begin to think about the impact we could make in the lions' dens of our lives. If, with the majesty, confidence, and dignity of Esther, we approached the lions and asked them to dinner, would they refuse us?

PRAYER

Thank you, God, for the magnificent picture of Esther that is painted in your Word. Thank you for her example of courage and grace. Teach me to approach difficult situations with that same kind of strength. Help me not be afraid to ask the kings and lions in my life to dinner. Amen.

FOLLOW-UP

Identify a person who is associated with a lion's den in your life. Pray for the strength and courage to ask the person for coffee, lunch, or dinner. Talk and listen honestly with the courage and grace of Esther.

eating pie

READ ESTHER 5:9-14 & MATTHEW 20:20-28.

Ever been bit by a "wanna bee"? If you have, you know all about their ability to get under the skin, buzz their way to the chest or head, and inflate an unsuspecting ego to two or three times its normal size. A "wanna bee" bite is a strange phenomenon that can cause delusions, leading to fierce, violent acts of boldness and false illusions of greatness.

"If onlys" are closely related to "wanna bees." They also are obnoxious little mites that burrow into the mind and distort the vision of their hosts. These little pests can cause inconsequential road bumps to look like enormous roadblocks. They can warp one's perspective so badly that trivial flaws may become debilitating handicaps. They can even cause friends to be misrepresented as adversaries. Once "if onlys" have a firm hold, things just don't look the same.

Both "wanna bees" and "if onlys" can cause destruction and ruin in individuals and in families. After the victim is infested by them, arrogance and misplaced pride can take over. Being right becomes absolutely essential to the infected person's self-esteem.

Haman had a bad case of "wanna bees" and "if onlys." He wanted to be the most important, most influential person next to the king. And he thought he was well on his way there. The buttons were just about popping from his chest as he proudly told his wife and family that he had been promoted above all the other nobles and officials. And he was the only person who Queen Esther had invited to dinner—not once but twice.

But Haman had a problem. One obstacle stood in the way of his complete and total satisfaction. "If only that disrespectful, good-for-nothing Jew would bow before me," Haman complained to his family, "then I would be happy. My success means nothing if I still have to look at him sitting at the king's gate."

Haman's wife suggested a plan for getting rid of Mordecai, and her idea made Haman smile. That very day he ordered his servants to build a large gallows, and he began his plotting for Mordecai's death. Haman was sure that once Mordecai was out of the way, he would find peace and contentment.

Other people in the Bible were bitten by "wanna bees" and "if onlys" too—and they weren't all villains like Haman. The mother of two of Jesus' disciples, James and John, wanted Jesus' assurance that her sons would have the most important places in Jesus' kingdom. And James and John went along with her plan. They were convinced they could follow Jesus in every way—enduring all the things he would endure. Their pride encouraged them to believe that was possible.

It's easy for us to look at Haman, James, and John and say, "What fools." It's easy to laugh at them and their vanity; when I do, I have to admit that I have also been bitten. When I look candidly at my own life, I know that there are "wanna bees" and "if onlys" there. If I am honest with myself, I know that pride also inflates my ego and makes me want to be the best and the most important. In my mind, I also entertain, "If only I could have my way of doing things, everything would be OK and I'd feel better" thoughts. I know that when I think that I'm better than Haman, or anyone else, I am the arrogant one.

These are the times I need to remember that Jesus gave us a recipe for "Humble Pie"—the perfect antidote for the "wanna bees" and "if onlys." He said, "whoever wants to become great among you must be your servant, and whoever wants to be first must be your slave" (Matt. 20:26-27). It's not difficult to understand why this is not a popular concept. Being a servant or slave means putting others first; it means giving to others selflessly. If Haman had gone home to his wife and dined on Humble Pie, he would not have wanted or needed anyone to bow to him. He would have known that he really wasn't very important in the greater scheme of things. He would have wanted to serve his fellow human beings, not hunt them down.

Bon appetit!

PRAYER

Thank you, Jesus, for the recipe for humility in your Word. Help me to be able to digest what this means for me. Teach me to be willing to serve you and those around me. Forgive me when pride dictates my actions. Amen.

FOLLOW-UP

Serve yourself a slice of Humble Pie. Then, be a servant to another person in a concrete, meaningful way.

no coincidence

READ ESTHER 6:1-5 & PSALM 23.

Drifting between the conscious and the darkness of the unknown, Susan lay in her hospital bed trying to remember her childhood. In her mind's eye she was transported back to the small but neat house with its white picket fence. That fence—the hint of a smile crossed her face as she remembered how, like Tom Sawyer, she had tricked her brother into painting it. Poor Tim. How he had cried when he discovered the hoax. Maybe it was then that she had decided to hate fences and tears.

So she had done without both in her life. She had decided to be totally free. But somehow she had never really tasted the satisfaction that she thought freedom would bring, until . . . The cobwebs that clouded Susan's brain could never be woven tightly enough to overshadow the memory of her first needle. She had soared like an eagle to unknown heights. For the first time in her life she believed that she had rid herself of the fences and the tears.

The ecstasy that she feasted on became the agony that choked her when she woke to the realization that she had become her own stunted cage. In her anguish she cried bitter tears.

Then, in a final frantic effort she reached again in desperate anticipation for the ultimate stimulation of the needle. But she failed, and now lying there, she did not know how to cope with the barricade of the hospital bed or with her own emptiness. The liberty of her life did not offer her any security or knowledge of how to deal with the confines of death.

In that final moment another memory crept into her mind. She was a small girl, and she could see her mother sitting on the side of her bed. She was softly reading, almost singing something. "The Lord is my shepherd, I shall not want." As Susan began to drift into the realm of another world, she reached out her hand, and her heart started to whisper the words. . . .

The death that my friend Susan faced seemed as inevitable as the destruction of the Jews in Susa. She had run away, and there was no place left to hide. Death stood ready to claim her. There was also little hope that disaster could be avoided for Mordecai. The gallows were built, the law etched in stone.

Mordecai and Susan faced certain death until God stepped into the picture. For Susan, God directed a restless intern who was roaming the hospital halls to hear her moans and keep vigil at her bedside through the long dark night. For Mordecai it was a sleepless king with a uneasy conscience who had a sudden unusual desire to be read the history books.

The intern strained to listen to what Susan was moaning. She recognized the words of Psalm 23 and began to recite them to Susan. Over and over the intern said the psalm, not knowing if Susan heard. Twice when Susan's heart stopped beating, the intern stubbornly restarted it. The nurses who assisted her thought Susan's life was a lost cause. But the young, naive intern refused to let her go.

In the king's bedroom the eunuchs read the old records, wondering why Xerxes wanted to hear all this history in the middle of the night. The king didn't say much, and the readers hoped he would soon fall asleep. Suddenly the king sat up straight. "This man, Mordecai—he saved my life five years ago. What honor and recognition did he receive?" the king asked. "I can't understand why he wasn't rewarded at the time. Is there anyone in the court?"

Poor Haman. He was probably making a lot of noise as he was building the gallows and impatiently anticipating Mordecai's hanging. Eagerly he came when the king called. Little things that might appear to be coincidences to an unknowing onlooker are the hand of God at work protecting his own.

As dawn began to break, Susan opened her eyes; tears of joy flowed freely. The fences were gone. She understood that she had been at death's door. She recognized that it was no chance happening that the young doctor who sat at her side knew the twenty-third psalm. Susan squeezed the intern's hand and whispered, "He told me that I'm ready to know him now."

When things couldn't get any worse for Esther, Mordecai, Susan—and for you and me—God is there. It's no coincidence.

PRAYER

Thank you for the knowledge that you will look after your children. Thank you for being in charge of my life. Help me to see your hand protecting me. Teach me to give you the credit for the blessings in my life. Thank you, Jesus, for loving me, even when I feel like a lost cause. Amen.

FOLLOW-UP

Think about a time in your life when you were sure things couldn't get much worse. Write a letter, thanking God for looking after you during that difficult time. Share your experience with a friend who is going through a difficult time.

getting what we deserve

READ ESTHER 6:6-14 & 1 CORINTHIANS 4:1-5.

Can you imagine the look on Haman's face? He had been almost drunk with the excitement of Mordecai's hanging when the king called him into the palace and asked his advice. Believing that he was the man the king wanted to honor, Haman described in detail his own dreams about how he would like to be treated. He would wear one of the king's own robes; that would really show everyone that the king respected him. He would also ride the king's horse, with the royal crest on its head. And one of the king's most noble princes would lead him through the streets proclaiming, "This is what is done for the man the king delights to honor!" When Xerxes told Haman to do all of the above for Mordecai, he must have had to find a chair to sit down and catch his breath.

Instead of watching his enemy die, Haman walked through Susa as Mordecai's servant. He must have choked on the words of honor and praise as he spoke them over and over again. When he was finished with this completely demoralizing and humiliating task, he hurried home to his wife and friends. It was obvious to them that after this unexpected turn of events,

it would not be in Haman's best interest to pursue Mordecai's demise. Unfortunately, before he could change his action plan, he was whisked away to Esther's banquet by the king's eunuchs. I don't think he felt much like eating by this time, but standing up the king would be unthinkable.

Haman had done the right things for the wrong reasons. Having his devious actions revealed must have been devastating for him.

The same thing sometimes happens today. Respected people suddenly fall from grace because some skeleton from their past comes out of the closet to haunt them. When a person we admire and respect is exposed as a fraud, it can be devastating.

We live in a society where many things are phony. Simulated leather, fun fur, and artificial sweetener are just a few of the imitations that are all around us. Unfortunately, phoniness comes not only in the products we buy but also in the people we deal with.

We're guilty of it too. If we treat people with great respect to their faces and then whisper something not so nice behind their backs, we are being fraudulent. Then our actions, like Haman's, have no merit.

It is important to us that people be authentic and real, that the love and compliments they offer us are genuine. Haman didn't care much about the well-being of others, especially the Jews, but he knew exactly what he wanted for his life. Haman only honored Mordecai because he had to. There was no love or respect involved.

This generation has sometimes been called the "Me Generation." People are perceived to have a "what's in it for me" attitude. Sometimes I see that attitude in my students at school. Rather than doing something just for the love of learning, they want to know how it will help their grade, how many points it's worth. I see it in the adults I know too. Most of us, at times, expect to earn good marks for doing good work.

When the report cards for our lives are handed out, our grades will depend on our incentive and reasons for the things we did. If our actions have been counterfeit, we, like Haman, will not receive a passing grade. If Christian love has driven our deeds, we will have a card filled with straight A's!

Our God knows what our motives are and will expose them. We will be rewarded for making love a selfless action word.

PRAYER

Jesus, thank you for the assurance that you know what's in my heart. Help me to be genuine in my service and caring for others. Give me the courage to be real sugar, not an artificial sweetener. Forgive me when my words or actions are not driven by your love. Amen.

FOLLOW-UP

Ask a friend or acquaintance who may be going through a difficult time, "How are you?" Ask it like you mean it. Show the person that you truly care about her/him. Commit to using the expression only if you really want to know how someone is.

staying warm

READ ESTHER 7 & MARK 4:35-41.

North Wind,

you bully us with your brutal, bitter beatings.
Yes, you can blow and break and bend.
You beat our brows and chill us to our bones;
*   you may even paralyze our frames.*
But you must be content with that,
*   for you cannot freeze us out.*
Don't you realize that your horrible howling
but helps us to recall the happier hours
*   of balmy breezes blowing*
*   gently through better days?*
Can't you see that your fierce force,
rattling our shutters, serves but to remind us
*   of a stronger strength than yours?*
For your careless cruelty will be surpassed
and leave you cold and friendless,

North Wind.

Esther could hear the wind howling, rattling her shutters, as she pleaded with Xerxes to spare her people from certain destruction. When he asked Esther who would dare to destroy his wife and her people, she answered, "The adversary and the enemy is this vile Hamen." Now it was Xerxes' turn to be shocked. He put down his wine and went into the garden to think.

Haman knew that he was now completely alone and friendless. He had worked so hard to get what he wanted, and now it was all gone. So this vicious, cruel man fell at the feet of a woman who would have been one of his victims, and he begged for his life. When Xerxes came back and thought that Haman was trying to molest his wife, the final irony happened. Xerxes became the cold, brutal north wind that howled at Haman. The eunuch covered Haman's face; he was a dead man. The force of Xerxes' anger had unleashed another tempest that was more powerful and brutal than Haman's own. Haman would be sucked into the cyclone of Xerxes' wrath and die a callous, frigid death.

On a stormy sea many years later, a small, crowded boat was in danger of being overturned by a vicious storm that yelled and howled. It chilled the passengers to their bones.

The captain of the ship was sound asleep while his worried crew feared for their lives. When Jesus was awakened by their terror, he ordered the storm to stop. He also reprimanded his followers for not having enough faith, for not believing that he was in charge of them and of the chaos that threatened to overcome them.

Haman's name could be substituted for the north wind in the poem. We could probably also substitute the name of a villain in our lives who daunts our hearts, our minds, or even our bodies. Faced with such a villain, we may feel as frightened as Esther did when her life and her people were threatened or as terrified as the helpless disciples in the boat. The wind can be scary, and it can be very, very cold. It may be strong enough to uproot us; it may blow and break and bend and paralyze our frames.

As surely as the seasons change, there will be cold, north winds that blow into our lives to torment and intimidate us. Our incredible assurance and confidence is the knowledge that no matter how insufferable it gets, the careless cruelty of the villain is subservient to a greater power: a Christ who will still the storm.

How wonderful to know that Jesus will keep us safe and warm us in the peace of his love!

PRAYER

I am so thankful, Lord, that you control the north wind. When it blows and howls, help me not to be afraid. Teach me to look to you for comfort and support when it threatens to break me. Give me the courage to acknowledge you to the villains in my life. Amen.

FOLLOW-UP

Turn on a fan and let it blow on you. Let it mess up your hair and make you feel cold. Then turn it off, reminding yourself that in the same way God controls the north winds that will blow into your life. Repeat the exercise when you are feeling threatened or overcome by storms.

decisions and socks

READ ESTHER 8:1-6 & LUKE 10:25-37.

Do you know how hard it is to turn socks the right way after they have been washed and dried? My children were forever putting socks into the wash all scrunched up and inside out. I complained and scolded for a long time about their thoughtlessness. I told myself that I grumbled because socks washed better turned the right way, but it was really because I resented doing it. I believed everyone in my family was old enough to take responsibility for turning their own socks.

It finally dawned on me that all my energy was being wasted. Nobody responded because they knew I would keep turning the socks anyway. One day I decided to try a new approach. I made a major announcement that I would do no more sock turning. The socks would come out of the laundry the same way they went in. Inside-out socks were no longer going to be my problem.

Socks really are not all that important. They're just one of many little things that I had to make a decision about. I could choose to be concerned about them, or I could choose to ignore them. But socks remind me that I have to make choices about the way I spend my time and about the things I do.

After Haman's death, Esther could have been content with having saved herself and her family, but she chose to risk her life again to plead for her people. She fell at the feet of Xerxes and begged him to write a law that would overrule the previous law. She knew that the law for destruction could not be changed. Once they were decreed, Persian laws were irrevocable. So, very carefully and properly, she asked the king to make another law that would allow her people to protect themselves.

Esther no longer had to worry about her life. The king had given her Haman's entire estate. Esther was now a rich woman in her own right. No one in their right mind would think of killing her on the twelfth of Adar (the day the Jews were going to be eliminated). Mordecai was safe as well, since he now wore the king's signet ring as a symbol of his importance to Xerxes. People wouldn't dare to harm him. So Esther and her family could be confident that they would not be harmed.

Under the circumstances, Esther could easily have found excuses not to endanger her life again. But instead she carefully thought and planned a way that she could be of service to her nation.

That kind of courage is seldom required or expected from us, but the fact remains that as we travel through life, we need to make decisions about the things we do. The choices we face may range from the relatively unimportant task of turning socks to important decisions about what we will do with our lives.

Many women today work outside of the home, so time is often limited and precious. Most women who work are also the primary caregivers for their children and the person in the family who carries the most responsibility for running the home. So what little spare time we have is precious, and it must be planned and used carefully. In the busyness of our lives, it may be tempting to cross the road so we don't see the stranger that may need us. It's tempting to say, "It's not my problem" and walk away. Although this may be understandable, it is not Christlike.

Esther had to make a difficult, important decison about what to do with her life. She prayed about it; she planned it; and she committed herself to doing it. We also need to find the time and the courage to make the right choices and decisions about what we will do with our lives. With God's help Esther was able to say, "It's my problem." Because she chose to deal with the problem, she became a blessing to her people and to us. You and I can be a blessing too. That's God's promise.

By the way, things are a lot better at my house in the sock department these days. My kids are older and wiser now. And so am I. Now there are days when I turn their socks, and there are days when I don't.

PRAYER

Jesus, thank you for the people that I can serve by turning their socks. Help me to take the time to make good decisions about my life. Enable me to see the stranger on the side of the road. Grant me the strength to offer my hand and myself. Amen.

FOLLOW-UP

Ask God to help you make a decision about a problem that you have been avoiding. (It could be as simple as turning socks or as difficult as making a career choice.) Make a list of different ways of addressing the challenge of the problem. Make a decision about the problem, and follow through on it.

maryann and her cows

READ ESTHER 8:7-14 & 2 THESSALONIANS 2:13-16.

There are cows everywhere in my friend's kitchen. They enhance the wallpaper, the canisters, the coffee mugs, and almost everything else in sight. Since hers is a large country kitchen on a dairy farm, the cows seem appropriate and fitting. They add to the warmth of the kitchen, a place where one can sit and enjoy friendship for long, calm hours, away from the noise and commotion of life in the city.

But last time I visited there, I couldn't resist looking for a metaphor in the cows. So I asked MaryAnn what special significance there was in having them as a focus of the decor. She laughed and said, "They're just cows. I like cows." "That's great," I said. "I like cows too, but I don't have them spread all over my kitchen." She went on to explain that people had started giving the cows to her as gifts, and the idea grew to fill her entire kitchen. The cows have become a symbol for the affection and friendship that many people have for her.

That's when it dawned on me that the comparison I was looking for in MaryAnn's kitchen should be centered not on her cows, but on her. I am reluctant to jeopardize our friendship by saying that MaryAnn is like a cow. However, she does model some cowlike behaviors. Cows stand in the meadow enduring a thunderstorm and remain seemingly unaffected. At the end of the afternoon they always return to the barn to give generously of themselves.

MaryAnn is a strong, Christian woman who stands secure and firm in an often inhospitable, hostile world. When the rains and storms of life beat down, she remains resolute and finds shelter in the unpretentious haven of her faith. When others graze in lonely meadows, she is the first one there with an umbrella to shield them from the attack of a storm. She gives selflessly of herself and sometimes gets soaked doing it.

There are times when MaryAnn too must be encouraged. At those times, standing steadfastly means accepting the support of others—sometimes in the form of a "cow" gift!

MaryAnn's feet are planted in solid foundations of stone, but that does not mean that she never sways or falters. I believe it is her resoluteness that enables her not only to befriend others relentlessly, but also to allow them to hold her up when she is tired or worn down.

The Jews in the Persian Empire received a reprieve from the slaughter that they were expecting. It came in the form of a law that said they could protect themselves against the onslaught of their enemies. They could get together, arm themselves, and even plunder the homes of their attackers. They were encouraged to be ready, to stand firm against their assailants. I'm sure a sigh of relief went up collectively to heaven. Families got together to plan how they would keep their weaker members safe.

For the Jews, standing firm did not mean doing nothing. To survive, people needed to act together to brace and defend themselves against their assailants. I'm sure there was great consolation in those endeavors—a feeling of togetherness that reassured and comforted those who were terrified about what the future held. For those who were so afraid and alone, I'm sure it must have felt something like it does to sit in the safety of MaryAnn's kitchen.

Sometimes possessions or things remind us of friends like MaryAnn who are resolute in their faith and commitment to others. The knowledge and assurance that ardent, strong friends are willing to sustain and uphold us with prayers and with words and acts of encouragement can shelter us against the chaos that threatens us during difficult, stressful times. These friends are special gifts from God. Together we must stand steadfast, determined to hold each other up.

When I see cows, I thank God for the MaryAnns in my life.

PRAYER

Thank you, Jesus, for providing friends who support and encourage me. Help me to appreciate them for the special people they are. Teach me how to know when they need to have their day brightened. Help me to be the kind of friend that you are to me. Amen.

FOLLOW-UP

Identify a person who you think of as being firm and secure in her/his faith. Send a card or write a note to the person, thanking her/him for the blessing that s/he provides for others. Watch for a time that you can support the person in a meaningful way.

singing in the streets

READ ESTHER 8:15-17 & PSALM 46.

"Did I ever tell you that my father's father's father married Judith, a Jewish girl who was brought here when we invaded Israel? I guess I never dared talk about it before. After all, Jews weren't very popular around here. But things have sure changed! After all, our queen is a Hebrew. And I'm proud that I'm one too. . . ."

What a difference a few days made in the city of Susa. One day the Jewish people were doomed, the next they were on top of the world. Instead of being ashamed of their Jewish roots, they were proclaiming them on the street corners.

The Jews beamed with pride as they saw Mordecai, one of their own, wearing the king's royal garments. There was no longer a reason to hide or pretend. After the fear they had lived through in the past few months, it felt right to revel in their heritage. It felt good to be respected, even feared, among the Babylonians. They had cause for great rejoicing!

During their feasting, they must have sung familiar songs. There was no synagogue for them to worship in, so the celebrations took place in the streets. It must have felt good to rejoice together, to sing the old songs, to tell the old stories about Abraham, Isaac, and Jacob, and to talk about the day they would be a nation again. The Hebrews understood what it meant to be delivered, and they knew how to praise God.

In some countries, God's people still live in the fear that they will be discovered for who they are. They meet in secret and keep their identity hidden for fear of the reprisal of the state. Like the Jews in Persia, they could face severe consequences for belonging to a church.

You and I are blessed to live in lands that offer us the liberty to worship however we wish. Yet with all the freedom we enjoy, sometimes we are still in hiding, afraid of what our friends will say or think of us.

In our community, there are times when we have ecumenical church services. Sometimes I am surprised at who I meet there. I suspect others are surprised to see me too. It's not hard to sing out the praises of our Lord at a church service; it feels good. To be together with God's people in God's house can encourage and strengthen us. For me, the hard part comes on Monday morning when I go to work. When the conversation gets around to what we did on the weekend, I am ashamed to tell you that there are times I don't mention the blessing I received from being in church.

From Esther and Mordecai, we can learn to acknowledge our faith publicly, even when it's not popular. Then, we will be able to sing joyfully with the people of God in our churches or alone in the busy streets of our lives. We will be able to sing the words of Psalm 46, written long after the Jews celebrated in Susa:

> "The Lord Almighty is with us;
> The God of Jacob is our fortress."
> —Psalm 46:11

PRAYER

Thank you, Lord, for the wonderful example of Esther and Mordecai in your Word. Give me the courage to sing your songs in my workplace and my play places. Strengthen me so that I will acknowledge you to my friends. Teach me not to fear what others will say about me. Amen.

FOLLOW-UP

Share with a friend the blessing you receive from going to church. Invite that person to worship with you the next time you go to church.

taking no plunder

READ ESTHER 9:1-10 & LUKE 6:27-36.

Julie often recited the rhyme, "Sticks and stones may break my bones, but names can never harm me." You and I both know that this verse is a lie. Names hurt a lot. Julie knew it too. When George, the playground bully, called her "fatty four eyes," she fought to hold back the tears that wanted to escape from her heart and the big blue eyes that peered out through her glasses. Often she would protect herself by seeking out a teacher and holding her hand as she walked around and monitored the playground. When the teacher would ask Julie if anyone had bothered her, she'd say, "You know the sticks and stones stuff, teacher." Although a faint smile would cross her face, her pain was obvious; the words were only a bandage.

The staff on yard duty always kept a close lookout for Julie. Part of the problem seemed to be that she was such an easy target. She never fought back. Of course, George was disciplined and spoken to about the way he harassed Julie, but it seemed to make no difference. He appeared to take real pleasure in pestering her. And she tried unsuccessfully to stay away from him.

Once George was heard commenting to his friends, "I want to make the little sissy cry. Then, maybe I'll stop bugging her."

I have to admit that I hated what George did to Julie. She was a sweet, simple child who did nothing to deserve such horrible abuse. I prayed that he would stop trying to hurt her. My prayers were answered, but it was in a very strange, unusual way.

It was a beautiful spring morning. The playground was filled with the happy noises of children playing. Suddenly, there was the shrill cry of "Fight! Fight!" from the far end of the yard. By the time I arrived at the spot, the fight was over. On the ground lay George. He was crying uncontrollably. In his hands he held what was left of his new glasses. Much to my surprise, Julie had arrived before me, and she was on the ground with her arm around George.

Everyone knew how George had treated Julie in the past. So we were amazed to hear her say, "Come on, George, I'll help you get up. Don't worry about that guy; he's just a bully who makes himself feel better by picking on someone smaller." As the words tumbled out of her mouth, Julie started to cry. George's mouth literally dropped open. And then he allowed Julie to help him up. The two children stood weeping and hugging each other.

Those who watched the heart-wrenching scene knew instinctively that something very unique was happening. Several of us cried with Julie and George. I think we sensed that a miracle was taking place.

Later we learned that George had responded to an older child who had teased him about his new glasses. George knew of only one way to defend himself. When his self-esteem was attacked, he lashed out in anger. Julie had understood his pain. I think her tears were for herself as much as for George. After that day, George became Julie's friend, and no one ever bothered her again.

On the thirteenth day of Adar the enemies of the Jews hoped to destroy them, but the tables were now turned. The Jews were the ones with the power. They could inflict the pain. They had been given the right to protect themselves—to destroy, kill, and annihilate anyone who dared attack them. They could also take the wives and children and plunder the property of their opponents. They could get mad. They could get even.

The Jews protected themselves, but they did not take any plunder. They did not know the teaching of Jesus about loving your enemies. They *did* know that there had to be a difference between how their enemies behaved and how they reacted.

When I asked Julie about why she had been so kind to George, she simply said, "I learned in church school that Jesus wants us to treat other people the way we want to be treated." I knew the verses from Luke 6 about loving your enemies. A seven-year-old child powerfully demonstrated to her peers and teachers what those verses meant.

Julie taught me that as hard as it may be not to take any plunder or to get even when the tables are turned, our response is a reflection of who we are.

PRAYER

Thank you, Jesus, for showing me how to love my enemies. Thank you for completely understanding how it feels to be hurt. Give me the strength to turn the other cheek when I am attacked. Teach me to protect myself with your love. Amen.

FOLLOW-UP

Think about a person who has hurt you. Identify a way that you could show the person Jesus' love. Pray for the strength to concretely show that love.

destroying a tapeworm

READ ESTHER 9:11-17 & ROMANS 12:9-21.

The shoes she had pitched through the window lay mutely in the middle of a sea of glass. Jane had come home unexpectedly from her trip. When she found her husband in bed with another woman, a terror and anger from some unknown place in her erupted. As the exposed couple prepared to make a hurried exit, she picked up their shoes, aimed, and threw them through the large picture window. The shattered glass was clearly symbolic of her life. It lay splintered and broken at her feet.

Jane's immediate impulse was to get revenge. She wanted to hurt her husband like he had hurt her. She knew that smashing the window was a stupid thing to do. It didn't even make her feel any better. But it did make her realize that she hated her husband for what he had done. She wondered if it was her way of telling him that their marriage was over.

This was not the first time that he had been unfaithful to her. She had forgiven him in the past, and she had worked hard to resolve their differences. But this time was different. She could no longer accept or condone the blatant contempt he had for their wedding vows.

As Jane began the unpleasant job of cleaning up the broken glass, she realized that it was the feeling of failure that consumed her. Everything she had been taught and believed said it was wrong for her marriage to end. Yet looking at the many splinters of glass, she knew that it *was* over. The time had come for her to be released from the pain and suffering of her marriage and of her own feelings of anger and defeat.

But she also knew that she must sweep away the thoughts of retaliation from her mind. She understood that the only way she could go on was to be released from the anger that held her in its grip. As she dropped to her knees, she sent up a voiceless, wordless prayer, begging for liberation from the emotions that threatened to devour her.

The Jews in Persia gathered together to protect themselves and to gain relief from those who threatened and oppressed them. To do that they had to kill seventy-five thousand of their enemies. In Susa five hundred men were killed, including the ten sons of Haman. Esther made the rather strange request that Haman's dead sons be hung on the gallows. Perhaps she did so to show the Jews and all the other people of Susa that the confrontation was really over. Haman, his family, and their ideals had been terminated. It's hard to imagine that all that killing was accomplished without anger or vengeance, yet we are told again that the Jews took no plunder.

Jane was faced with the injustice of a husband's infidelity. She smashed a window to show that she could no longer tolerate it. The Jews killed their oppressors to save their nation from being destroyed. The anger that the Jews and Jane must have felt is undeniable and understandable, I think. Perhaps even righteous. Coming to terms with it and dealing with it were important parts of being able to let it go.

Anger is an emotion that has to be dealt with. It's like a tapeworm that must be coaxed out into the light to be seen and then destroyed. Each of us must deal with the feeling of being consumed by anger at some point in our lives. We may face the pain of physical, mental, emotional, or spiritual abuse; the inequity of a child killed by a drunk driver; or the unfairness of contacting AIDS. The anger that we feel in such a situation can fester and eat away at our souls. Then, like Jane, we may need to expose and face our feelings and let the healing balm of God's grace soothe the brokenness.

In the darkest times and days of our lives, it may be tempting to take revenge on those who have tormented us and caused suffering and pain; but God tells us that he will take revenge on our enemies.

It couldn't have been easy for the Jews in Susa not to want to punish those who were going to take such pleasure in killing them. I know it wasn't easy for Jane not to retaliate. When we are in similar situations, it will probably also be a struggle for us.

We are blessed to serve a Savior who has shown us how it's done!

PRAYER

Thank you, Jesus, for dying for me. Thank you for your perfect example of how to stay calm under difficult circumstances. Help me to recognize what my emotions are and then teach me how to deal with them constructively. Give me the wisdom and courage to overcome evil with good. Amen.

FOLLOW-UP

On a sheet of paper write in large letters a painful experience that has been difficult for you to let go. Take the experience to Jesus and pray that he will allow you to let it go. Cut up the paper and trash it. Believe that it is now in God's hands.

peanut butter sandwiches

READ ESTHER 9:18-22 & MATTHEW 14:13-21.

Our fussy eater always looked forward to his birthday. For him that was "no-veggie" day, the day he got to choose whatever he wanted for dinner.

Allowing the birthday person to select his or her favorite foods has led to some unusual meals for our family. Once we had peanut butter and jelly sandwiches and chocolate cake and ice cream. It was a real celebration for a child who hated vegetables! For the rest of us, it was an unusual reminder that special means different things to different people. And although it was remarkably easy to prepare, that peanut butter and jelly feast was one of the most memorable birthday dinners our family has ever shared.

It is interesting that all of the important events in the book of Esther happened around banquets. At the beginning of the story the lavish extravagance of Xerxes' banquet prompted him to make an unreasonable request that provided the setting for Queen Vashti's defiance. Later, the new queen, Esther, used banquets to make her wishes known to Xerxes.

The palace wasn't the only place where food and meals played an important role. The Jews often used food to celebrate. So it is not surprising that the miraculous deliverance of the people of God in Persia called for a day of feasting and joy. What would have been a day of mourning without divine intervention became "a day of joy and feasting, a day for giving presents to each other."

Notice the contrast between the banquet that the book of Esther starts with and the feasting that the Jews took part in after their deliverance. Xerxes celebrated his own accomplishments while the Jews gave thanks to God by giving gifts to the poor. The gratitude and joy that people felt for being delivered was extended to those who were less fortunate. (I'd like to believe that poor Persians were also the recipients of the gifts that were given.)

When the crowds who followed Jesus to hear his message and receive his blessing got hungry, he fed them with a little boy's lunch. It was a simple meal of bread and fish, but it was also a grand banquet spread on a tablecloth of grass. I'm sure it was a meal that the participants never forgot. They must have felt a special bond after listening to Jesus and then taking part in the miracle feast that he provided.

In the Bible food plays an important part in commemorating particularly important events in the history of our faith. The Old Testament Jews celebrated the Passover, a feast that reminded them of how they had been delivered from slavery in Egypt. In the New Testament, Jesus established the Lord's Supper as a celebration and reminder of how he set us free for all eternity. Our religious feasts, as well as our family meals, are times when we share community. They are an important part of being together.

For the Jews in the streets of Susa and for the followers of Jesus on the shores of the Sea of Galilee, sharing food and fellowship was a significant way to be part of a community of believers. Although some of our customs and observances are much different from those of the people of the Old and New Testaments, the importance of being together with people to celebrate has not changed over the centuries. Our special meals don't have to be fancy. They don't even have to include vegetables! Whether we feed our bodies with a peanut-butter-and-jam sandwich, a loaf of bread and a fish, or a magnificent gourmet dinner, it is important to remember that we also feed and nurture our souls when we "break bread" together.

PRAYER

Thank you, Lord, for the food you provide so generously for me. Thank you for opportunities to celebrate. Help me to make mealtimes a time to celebrate my family and friends. Teach me to build community in my life. Amen.

FOLLOW-UP

Talk to your family about the importance of eating together. Invite someone who usually eats alone to your house for dinner.

telling our stories

READ ESTHER 9:23-32 & PSALM 66:1-12.

"Your daughter drank half a bottle of cough syrup."

My father-in-law had passed away suddenly, and we were receiving family and friends at the funeral home. The baby-sitter's words on the phone seized us with terror. When the safety of our children is at risk, nothing else seems to matter.

We hurried home and rushed Beth to the hospital emergency. The doctor told us the cough syrup would have to come out immediately, and he gave Beth something to induce vomiting—something Beth later referred to as "maple syrup." Even though she was only two years old when it happened, she never forgot that horrific experience.

When Beth was three, she went to church school for the first time and heard the story about Martha and Mary. That story also stuck. When she came home, she christened two nameless dolls Martha and Mary. And she acted out the story repeatedly for her baby sister.

Then there was the story of *Curious George Goes to the Hospital*. When we read that book, there was no use trying to skip any pages to speed up the reading because Beth could recite it verbatim.

"Tell me the story again, Mommy," was a common request from Beth. Whether it was the story of Mary and Martha, of Curious George, or of the time she drank a bottle of cough syrup, the narratives had to be repeated over and over again. There were other stories she liked too, but it was these three that she wanted to hear regularly.

I often wondered what it was that kept Beth so fascinated with three different stories. Many years later she explained to me that all of the stories dealt with being taken care of. When she was at risk, the people she loved were there to look after her. When Jesus spoke up for Mary, he was looking after his friend in a real and meaningful way; Beth believed that he would do the same for her. And Curious George? "He reminded me of me," Beth explained. He was taken care of in the hospital and lovingly cared for in the same way she had been when her life was in danger.

In their own different ways the stories made Beth feel safe and secure. There was comfort and reassurance for her in knowing that Jesus, her parents, and others would look after her. She would never be alone.

Her explanation reminded me of the importance of remembering stories of God's goodness. When the Jews thought about how close they had come to dying, they rejoiced and celebrated. They understood what an important event had taken place, and they never wanted to forget what God had done for them. So they established the feast of Purim. Every year when they celebrated that feast, they would remember how God had used Esther and Mordecai to save the Hebrew people. They would tell their children and their children's children the story. When things looked bleak and discouraging for them, they would remember that God could and would look after them. That would help them to reaffirm their faith in God.

When we look ahead in our lives, there are many unknowns. Remembering and reflecting on the stories of the heroes of faith—from the Bible as well as from our own lives—can prepare us to move ahead. Of course, we still won't know what the future holds, but we can be assured that the faithfulness of the God of our mothers and fathers will inspire us with hope and perseverance to deal with the obstacles and difficulties that life may present.

Beth still likes old stories. Now they include many other stories of difficult times in our lives. When we tell the stories to each other, it is with a deep appreciation and understanding of the faithfulness of our God, who enables us to put past experiences to work for us in the present and who helps us to look with confidence to the future. Like the Jews who established the feast of Purim to remember the way their race had been saved, she and I know that we must not forget God's faithfulness in our daily lives. Telling and retelling each other our stories of God's providence helps us to remember.

PRAYER

God, thank you for your Word and the many stories of faith that I can read there. Thank you for my own stories of your faithfulness to me. When I feel discouraged, help me to remember and retell the stories of how you have been there for me. Give me the courage to live a life of faith. Amen.

FOLLOW-UP

Write down one of your own stories of how God has been there for you. Share it with a loved one. When you are feeling discouraged, read the story again and know that God will be with you.

happily forever after

READ ESTHER 10 & ROMANS 8:28-39.

The fire-breathing dragon is destroyed. The prince and princess confront many dangers, find each other at last, and live happily ever after. . . .

Sound familiar? That's pretty much the story line of most fairy tales. The hero overcomes the forces of the evil villain, and he and his true love live happily ever after. The hero is courageous, brave, kind, trustworthy, and loving. The villain reveals exactly the opposite qualities. In the end, good triumphs over evil.

It's not difficult to understand the appeal of fairy tales. We human beings like nothing better than to see the wicked villain annihilated. It makes most of us happy when things work out and people can live happy, contented, peaceful lives. That's how we would like our lives to be.

If we read chapter 10 of the book of Esther with unbelieving eyes, it might appear that the story of Esther and Mordecai concludes like a classic fairy tale. Mordecai was respected by everyone, and he continued to do good for his people. In effect he had slain the mighty Persian dragon who had tried to exterminate the Jews and now he ruled, second only to the mighty King Xerxes. It might appear that his heroism had made him the victor who, of course, was greatly honored for his courageous deeds.

Although Esther is not mentioned in the last chapter, we can assume that she also remained in favor with Xerxes and was looked up to in the same way that Mordecai was. It certainly looked like everyone was going to live happily for the rest of their lives.

And some people do view the book of Esther that way. It's nothing more, they say, than an interesting story about a hero and a villain. It has little religious value.

However, if we consider Esther and Mordecai heroes of faith, a different picture presents itself. As members of a chosen nation, Esther and Mordecai were a small part of a means to salvation that God first promised to Adam and Eve. Through Abraham and his twelve sons, the Hebrew nation was selected by God to bring a Savior who would redeem all the nations of the world. If that nation had been obliterated by the Persians or any other villain, God's plan for salvation would not be accomplished for the Jews—or for us.

God did not let that happen. The story of Esther is just one small part of a much larger account of how God is in control of history. God used heroes of faith like Esther and Mordecai to bring the promise of salvation to us.

The account of Esther and Mordecai is not a story of two perfect fairy-tale characters. It is a story of real people who made mistakes, but who through God's perfect plan were used as a blessing to their people. Unlike fairy-tale characters, Esther and Moredecai did not work things out themselves. They were chosen by God and were used to bring about God's purpose. Their strength came from God.

Notice too that Mordecai "kept working for the good of his people." He didn't quit after the danger was over. I think that at the end of the book he truly understood what it meant to be part of God's chosen people. He had learned to be open to letting God work in his life.

In the world that you and I live in there are powerful, dangerous, fire-breathing dragons who will try to harm us. The reality is that sometimes that dragon may indeed burn our house down, kill someone we love, or cause some other evil to befall us. Even when we are sure and secure in our faith, bad things may happen to us. Life will not always be fair. That is pretty much what Romans 8: 36 tells us: Just because we believe in God doesn't mean that everything will always be smooth and easy for us.

So most of us probably won't live fairy-tale lives. The Jews didn't either.

But like Esther and Mordecai, we must trust and believe that "God works for the good of those who love him, who have been called according to his purpose." We have the wonderful assurance that in God's time, our lives will be better than the best fairy tale. God will see to it that all the dragons are dead.

What a comfort it is to know that we will live happily forever after with God!

PRAYER

Thank you, Jesus, that you are more powerful than all the dragons of the world. Give me the strength and courage to keep fighting evil in my life. Help me to believe that whatever happens, you are in charge. I praise you for the assurance of spending eternity with you. Amen.

FOLLOW-UP

Identify a dragon in your life. Pray that God will give you the courage and faith to keep fighting it. Believe that God will overcome all the dragons in your life.